The Spokesman
Resist Much, Obey Little
A collection in honour of Ken Coates

Edited by Tony Simpson

Published by Spokesman for the
Bertrand Russell Peace Foundation
Ken Coates: Editor 1970 to 2010

Spokesman 116   2012

CONTENTS

Cover: *A painting by Piero Dorazio
(photo: Deborah and Tamara Coates)*

ISSN 1367 7748   Printed by the Russell Press Ltd., Nottingham, UK   ISBN 978 0 85124 814 1

Subscriptions
Institutions £35.00
Individuals £20.00 (UK)
        £25.00 (ex UK)

Back issues available
on request

A CIP catalogue record
for this book is available
from the British Library

Published by the
Bertrand Russell Peace
Foundation Ltd.,
Russell House
Bulwell Lane
Nottingham NG6 0BT
England
Tel. 0115 9784504
email:
elfeuro@compuserve.com
www.spokesmanbooks.com
www.russfound.org

FSC
Mixed Sources
Product group from well-managed
forests and other controlled sources

Cert no. SGS-COC-006541
www.fsc.org
© 1996 Forest Stewardship Council

Ken Coates

Editorial

Resist Much, Obey Little

We dedicate this issue of *The Spokesman* to Ken Coates, the journal's editor for forty years, from 1970 to 2010. During those decades he oversaw the publication of more than one hundred issues, notching up the ton in 2008 with this comment about the military industrial complex and NATO:

> 'If we continue to generate another hundred issues of this journal, while we have breath left, we shall resist these embodiments of militarism, and continue to devote our energies to laying the foundations of the peaceful commonwealth which will come into existence with the abolition of war.'

In *Spokesman 100*, Ken placed the emphasis on democracy, asking was it 'growing or dying?' In particular, he revisited democracy at work, which for him, as much as the causes of peace and poverty, was a persistent priority. Now, in a short memoir, written with characteristic clarity, he explains the links between his lifelong campaigns against poverty and for workers' control.

For a long time, Ken resisted many calls to write his memoirs. 'In the beginning was the deed,' was his approach, and he would write prolifically in support of a chosen course of action. Nevertheless, towards the end of his life, he did find time to compose his thoughts and recollections about how he came to leave the pit and go to university, and how work on material poverty fitted with his concerns about alienation, which in due course led to the emergence of the Institute for Workers' Control, or IWC, as it is popularly known.

So it is that we begin this little collection with two previously unpublished pieces from Ken's own hand. They may have been works in progress, but they have all the hallmarks and attributes of luminous Coates' prose. (Ken was very heartened when he heard that his friend, the playwright Trevor Griffiths, had said 'no one writes like Ken Coates'.)

Trevor urged Ken to record his memoirs, if he wasn't going to write them. Fortunately, George Lambie, recorder in hand, had approached Ken for an interview about his research into political developments in Britain during the 1970s. Their subsequent conversations probed the evolution of the IWC, including Tony Benn's participation; the origins of the Alternative Economic Strategy; Labour's 1973 Programme with its landmark industrial strategy; and Stuart Holland's pioneering work on European economic recovery, which, as readers of *The Spokesman* will know, continues to this day. But the discussion also ranged much more widely, to include European Nuclear Disarmament (END), Bukharin and China, and Cuba, as these exchanges reveal.

Michael Barratt Brown, John Daniels, Regan Scott and Bill Silburn add their own reflections about working with Ken Coates. Tony Benn generously gave of his time to be interviewed about his old comrade and friend. Ken Fleet helped edit the contributions; on a daily basis, he worked closely with Ken Coates for more than 40 years, following their initial meeting at the Workers' Educational Association in the 1960s.

Even so, the picture is very much a partial one. Whenever Ken Coates reviewed biographies of Bertrand Russell, with whom he worked closely in the last years of Russell's long life, he usually affirmed the need for more biographies of Russell. Similarly, we need more memoirs of Ken Coates, and cordially invite contributions.

Ken turned to Walt Whitman for the sub-title to his book about the divisions in Communism, *Heresies: Resist Much, Obey Little,* published in 1982. The poet's injunction resonates today, in much the same way as the causes of democracy and peace, which Ken espoused so eloquently for so long.

Tony Simpson

PS We have turned to William Blake, whose work Ken Coates loved, to help illustrate this collection. For our cover, we chose Piero Dorazio, a permanent favourite in the Coates household.

To the States, or any one of them, or any city of the States,
Resist much, obey little;
Once unquestioning obedience, once fully enslaved;
Once fully enslaved, no nation, state, city, of this earth,
    ever afterward resumes its liberty.

Walt Whitman: *Leaves of Grass*

Insistent Lad

Ken Coates

How did I move away from Bilsthorpe pit to become a student at Nottingham University? Part of the answer is to be found in the Workers' Educational Association in which I became a regular student. But miners work shifts, so that it was very difficult indeed to follow any extended course uninterruptedly. My salvation came when I was accepted as a student on the miners' day release courses, which were conducted jointly by the WEA and the University of Nottingham's Extra-mural Department. For two days a week, a term at a time, I became a student of Economic History, Logic, Economics and the mysteries of the English language. The two days included a Saturday, so that I was actually released from the pit one day a week, but attended the other under my own steam.

Not all the subjects were equally interesting, and Logic entailed the learning, parrot-wise, of various common fallacies, together with the labyrinthine medieval formulae concerning the figures of the syllogism. These involved the memorisation of a famous mnemonic. The first verse we owe to William of Sherwood who surely little expected, in the darkness of his distant time, that his incomprehensible song would be sung by Nottinghamshire miners:

> *'barbara, celarent, darii, ferio;*
> *cesare, camestres, festino, baroco;*
> *darapti, disamis, datisi, felapton,*
> *   bocardo and ferison;*
> *bramantip, camenes, dimaris, fesapo,*
> *   fresison.'*

Not many colliers enjoyed this lyric, and few mastered the skills of argument it summarised and concealed, although several had the natural endowment that enabled them to talk the hind legs off donkeys.

The idea that I might become a full-time university student was fostered by the young man who taught us Economic History, who appreciated my essays and sought to get me admitted to his old department at Sheffield University. I was accepted, but my interests proliferated, and I soon found myself more attracted to following an English course.

That became possible thanks to an Irishman. During these days, the BBC broadcast raw drama from Ireland, and one night I found myself listening to a play by Sean O'Casey called *Red Roses for Me*. It was about the adventures of a young man in the great Dublin strike wave, and I found it an electrifying experience. Sean O'Casey married severe realism to a wild sense of human potential. The strike became, in this crucible, not only a harrowing struggle, but also an extraordinary burst of hope and aspiration. O'Casey painted the prospect of a sunset over the River Liffey in which the entire city of Dublin was overwhelmed in a rage of colour. This was lovingly described by three flower sellers, and became an image of the world as it might be, clearly emerging from the troubles that presently possessed it. Another world, it seemed, was possible.

So I read O'Casey, and I read him again. The other great 'realistic' plays were easy to obtain: *Juno and the Paycock*, and *The Plough and the Stars*. I followed through the entire cycle of O'Casey's writing, including his remarkable six volumes of autobiography. Some time towards the end of this immersion, I plucked up the courage to write to the great man himself, and I sent him two letters, long since lost, to which he was kind enough to reply. Since then, David Krause has edited O'Casey's surviving letters in four volumes, the first of which won him a *Sunday Times* award for Book of the Year. So Krause has done me the favour of summarising my youthful letters as follows:

'I originally wrote to O'Casey to ask him his views on socialist realism, because I had been reading his work systematically, and had graduated from it to read Joyce. This had led me to the conclusion that O'Casey himself had nothing to do with socialist realism, and that if socialist realism had anything to do with art, it was purely accidental. His first reply clearly confirmed that he shared these views, so I wrote to him again, asking him why he did not express such opinions publicly, since if he and other great Communist artists like Brecht, Guttuso and Picasso were to speak up, the whole cramping, debilitating nonsense would be completely discredited. His second letter did not directly answer this question; but I read it as implying an answer, that if we "first removed the beam from our own eye" we should see that the enemy of art in Britain was not Zhdanov but the liberal establishment.'[1]

At this time it was suggested that I might usefully apply for a State Scholarship to enter the university. About a score of these were issued nationally every year, each based upon the submission of an essay and an interview. Because of my total immersion in the work of O'Casey I chose to write about him. My quite substantial judgement was sent off, and I had almost forgotten about it when I was summoned for interview at the Ministry of Education. The experience was not daunting, although I had expected it to be. We had a pleasant chat about what I had written, and I was flattered to understand that the panel had actually read my piece. Subsequently I was informed that the Scholarship had been awarded.

The officials at the pit surprised me greatly. My status heretofore had been that of resident subversive, and although I was tolerated, this was without enthusiasm. Of course the arguments inside the Communist Party were far removed from the Nottinghamshire coalfield, so that my somewhat anguished political evolution was a closed book, not only to my workmates but also to my bosses. So when I was sent for by the Manager, I wondered what trouble I was in this time. To my astonishment, he offered me his effusive congratulations. He knew that State Scholarships did not grow on trees and he was proud that one of his lads had been awarded one.

Suddenly, all the officials became friendly. The Training Officer called me in to his cubicle, and showed me the extensive file that the Coal Board had been nourishing over the years, concerning all my troubled past. When I was eighteen years old, I had been sacked from one pit after drafting a letter to the National Union of Mineworkers calling for the equalisation of juvenile wage rates between the areas of Derbyshire and Nottinghamshire. Lads under twenty-one were paid according to markedly different scales in the two Counties, and the Derbyshire youngsters were substantially worse off under this system. All the lads therefore signed my letter, and it went off to the Union. The next week I had been summoned by the under-manager, who explained to me that I could play ball with him if I chose, and I would secure rapid promotion to the coalface. But I could go my own way if I wished, and retribution would not be long delayed. Naively I had explained that I had done nothing wrong, and that the working of the pit would be improved if the wages system was reformed as I had suggested. This advice was not accepted.

A few days later I was sent to the job of driving a conveyer belt at some considerable distance from the coalface, and from all the other workers. My belt debouched on to another, and my task was to shovel up any coal that spilt to the ground during that transfer. Usually there was not much. But if the main conveyer stopped, and I was slow to switch off the subsidiary one, there could be quite a lot. But normally it was not an onerous task and on this morning I nodded off to sleep. The under-manager, riding down the belt, caught me, and sent me out of the pit. I was instantly dismissed. What I did not know then was that the bright young manager to whom he reported me had written a recommendation on my records, which now I was about to leave the industry, I was shown. 'Do not employ this man. He is a dangerous agitator.' So dangerous indeed, that he could be snuffed out without a murmur of protest at a moment's notice.

The only reason I had subsequently obtained employment at Bilsthorpe was that I had applied for jobs to several pits at the same time, and the damning records of my misdemeanours had been sent to another colliery, which had been slow in forwarding them on. So I got my new job, but was promptly placed on the socially devastating afternoon shift for a long time. The Training Officer should not have allowed me into the secrets of his files, but they did explain a number of events that had subsequently happened to me.

Leaving Bilsthorpe I was admitted to the English Department at Nottingham University. Two political events followed immediately. Britain joined with France and Israel in the Suez war, and the Russians invaded Hungary following an upsurge of political opposition. In England, demonstrations were everywhere. I felt that the study of the silver poets of the sixteenth century was a little distant from the intellectual problems to which I needed answers, and so it came about that I transferred my studies to courses on Sociology and Politics.

Two letters from Sean O'Casey[2]

To Ken Coates
1 JULY 1955
Dear Ken Coates,
You are a young miner, a Communist, and you want to write. Well, you couldn't want to do a worse thing. It is the most precarious of employments, without any chance of a dole. If you persist, then hold on to your job, and write in your hour of leisure; unless you can get another job that may be more suitable under the circumstances; but till you are sure of an alternative job, stick to the one you have. I couldn't say for certain that I could see you if you came down to Devon. That would all depend on the circumstances of the time; I have a lot to do between work and family affairs, and can't make definite arrangements to meet all who wish to come to see me. There has been a lot of 'Socialist' blather about 'socialist realism', without any who wrote about it having an idea of what it is or

what it meant. What is it, anyhow? Remember that Life comes first, even before socialism. A writer must write of the life around him; what he sees, feels, and hears, corresponding with life through his senses; there is no other way. And the life of England, of Ireland, Scotland, Wales, the Channel Islands, and the Isle of Man is a complex one, bewildering, lively, dull, selfish, generous, and so on. And what a complex thing is one human life alone! All it has to deal with, within himself, without from the life of others. Zhdanov – of whom you have heard, I daresay – didn't know what he was talking about; and all who echoed him in the *Daily Worker*, and elsewhere, knew a damned sight less. Read Harry Pollitt's writing, his 'diary' while he toured India, his biography, and, however good a lad he is – and he is clever, sincere, and good-hearted – he hasn't the faintest idea of how to do it, or anything but the faintest idea about literature in general. James Joyce would but irritate him; and the same can be said for 90% of the Communists of England. They are shamefully and shamelessly ignorant of their own greatness in the achievements of the English people. The Soviet Writers are realising all this now. The other week, a prominent Soviet Writer came here to discuss with me a proposal to publish in the USSR all my biographical books, which, alone, shows the change that has or is taking place there in literary thought and desire. I wonder how many 'communists' have read Strindberg's DREAM PLAY? Yet in this play, in a few lines, integral part of the drama, the dramatist proclaims the whole gospel of socialism. Again, Keats, who is never mentioned in the *Worker*, lets us know in fourteen lines the implication of all that Marx and Engels ever wrote.

The worst formalism that I know of is the formalism of the chattering phrases uttered and muttered by the Communists themselves.

The Communist must be interested in everything, must know something about everything; he must talk to the shepherd about sheep, the farmer about crops! I listen to the talk about farming problems on the BBC and Radio Eireann, whenever I get a chance – to the doctor about surgery and medicine, to the priest about religion, and to the worker about work. So, instead of going about always teaching, the Communist should be always going about learning. The Communists I have met, and I've met many, know too damned much, without knowing anything at all; a lot of them are the dullest humans imaginable; and do a tremendous lot of harm to the Communist cause.

And because of this ignorance, they do the most stupid things. They don't know how to talk about anything outside of a socialist pamphlet. They make me sick.

Robbie Burns was a communist of his day, but he had time and the desire to sing 'My love is like a red, red rose'.

THE FLYING WASP (1937) has been long out of print. The critics didn't like it, and no wonder. At the moment, oddly enough, I am going over it again, for it is to be published – or so the prospect goes – with other articles of mine, in a volume to be issued by a New York publisher. So one day – if your desires hold out – you may be able to get it after all.

Finally, for I am very busy, don't attempt to write, unless you feel an irresistible and insufferable desire to do so. Fight against the desire; but if it conquers, well, then, go ahead, in the name of God and Man; but hold on to a job till you KNOW that your work will bring in enough to keep you.

All good wishes to the young miner.

Yours very sincerely,

Sean O'Casey

To Ken Coates
17 JULY 1955
Dear Ken,

You are an insistent lad. Sorry, I didn't make my opinion clear in my last letter. Still, I'm not sure of what you want to know. First, I haven't the faintest idea of what "Socialist realism" is, and I don't think anyone else has either. I've read miles of opinions about it, from Zhdanov down to Howard Fast, and can't yet get the swing of it. I don't bother anyway to make sure, since I know something about the Realism and the Fantasy of life, which are more important than any theory. Yes, I agree that a lot of Communists are as dogmatic as any cleric; stupidly so; and I have had many a dose of boredom from them. But you have this ritualistic formulism or formalism among the liberal leaders of thought and literature here, just as many as in any other place. For instance, the Drama Critic of the TIMES LITERARY SUPPLEMENT said not long ago that 'the British People had decided to ignore O'Casey because of his lamentable judgements'. There's one for you. And, indeed, so they have, for it's little I get from them, three times more from Ireland, and as much from Israel and Germany; but 95% of what I get comes from the USA. What in hell have you got to do with Zhdanovism? Is England not big enough for You? The USSR has her own way of walking, thinking, and hoping, and the Soviet People must evolve from their own environment and activities; England from Her's, of which you are part. Communism will come, sooner or later, to all countries, but not necessarily in the same way everywhere.

It hasn't come to the USSR yet; but, I believe, it is on its good way. What remains for all is to live in peace, and for each to work out its own salvation in its own way; and that is the way things will have to go now, for force no longer can be used without wiping out everything – Communism included. Zhdanov is dead. Out of date now; and always was. But remember, the artist everywhere will have a hard task to get a living; good even if he gets a loaf, a flask of wine, and a girl. I myself have been condemned by most; after JUNO, the Sunday *Worker* in a letter referred to me as Judas; Mike Gold, a prominent Left-winger in USA, after WITHIN THE GATES appeared in New York, wrote a whole seething column of abuse; the other day, 20 years after, he wrote another one bubbling with praise. What do I care whether he praises or blames? He doesn't know a damn thing about literature or art. Read what Worsley said about SUNSET AND EVENING STAR. If these lads had the power that Zhdanov had, what would happen to us? Let us remove the beam from our own eye before we busy ourselves with the mote in our brother's. The USSR is now beginning to prepare for the translation of my work – after 30 years of friendship. I've never asked them to do it; or have I ever asked anyone to take an interest in me – bar once when more than 40 years ago I sent an effort to G.B.S. for his opinion, and got a reply! This I acted on – 'depend on yourself, and be published for your own sake' – I suggested he should write a preface! By the way, the finest collection of Picassos is in the USSR, whose collection of Modern Art – got when they hardly had a red rex (a penny) – is second to none. Brecht is, I think, now in Moscow. I had his manager here the other day, who told me his 'Ma Courage' is to be done there. The USSR has respect for Hauptman.

If you are going to write, write then, and don't bother about the gibbering Marx-theorists, who can prate like Poll, but don't understand in their minds what their mouths are spouting. This is the one and only way I suggest. You do as I do – if you write, write, and to hell with all opinions as to how you do it.

Are you doing N.Service in the mines? Must end now.

The God of Marx, Lenin, and Stalin (three geniuses) be with you.

Sean O'Casey

Footnotes
1 *The Letters of Sean O'Casey, Volume III 1955-1958*. Edited by David Krause, The Catholic University of America Press, Washington, D.C. pp. 157.
2 As above, pp. 157-9 and 163-4.

he promulgates his ten commands, glancing his heavy eyelids over the deep in dark dismay,

19. Where the son of fire in his eastern cloud, while the morning plumes her golden breast.

20. Spurning the clouds written with curses, stamps the stony law to dust, loosing the eternal horses from the dens of night, crying Empire is no more! and now the lion & wolf shall cease.

Chorus

Let the Priests of the Raven of dawn, no longer in deadly black, with hoarse note curse the sons of joy. Nor his accepted brethren whom, tyrant, he calls free: lay the bound or build the roof. Nor pale religious lechery call that virginity, that wishes but acts not!

For every thing that lives is Holy

13

Poverty and the IWC

Ken Coates

Empire is no more!
and now the lion & wolf
shall cease ...

◀ A Song of Liberty, *from the* Marriage of Heaven and Hell *by William Blake, which Ken Coates chose for the cover of his book,* Empire No More!

I spent a lot of time working on problems of poverty. Poverty was visible all around us in the 1960s and '70s, and became the object of a remarkable academic industry. Foremost among the scholars who initiated all this effort was Peter Townsend, who published a small brochure which detonated large explosions. *The Poor and the Poorest*, jointly written with Brian Abel-Smith, appeared in 1965. It offered a careful dissection of Ministry of Labour figures on household expenditure, and compared the actual incomes of people in 1953 and 1960 with the National Assistance scales which were operative at those times. Taking the official definitions, the authors found that 7.8 per cent of the population was living in poverty in 1953, and that the proportion was growing, so that by 1960, 14.2 per cent of the population was affected. This involved seven and a half million people, and the claim brought a decisive end to years of complacency about the material conditions of the British people.

I was teaching an adult class at Nottingham University at this time, and we looked at the findings of *The Poor and the Poorest* with some attention to detail. So impressed were my students that they decided to check out the work of these sociologists against actual conditions in an extended slum area of Nottingham, chosen because it began a short walk from the Adult Education Centre in which we were working. We recruited a second tutor, Richard or Bill Silburn, and started work. All that gave rise to a string of publications, and there is no need to rehearse them here. We conducted an extensive social survey over a number of years, and our findings amply confirmed those of our teachers, Townsend and Abel-Smith.

All that is summed up in our first report, which I prepared with Richard Silburn, *St. Ann's: Poverty, Deprivation and Morale in a Nottingham Community*, and in the subsequent book, published by Penguin, *Poverty: The Forgotten Englishmen*.

But these publications, and the attendant public agitation to which they gave rise, distracted me from the fundamental insight to which I was beginning to devote myself in those days. This considered poverty as by no means simply a lack of material resources but also as mainly a want of spiritual development. True, we quoted in *The Forgotten Englishmen*, the wise words of Bernard Shaw.

'Nothing, therefore, is really in question, or ever has been, but the differences between class incomes. Already there is economic equality between captains, and economic equality between cabin boys. What is at issue still is whether there shall be economic equality between captains and cabin boys. What would Jesus have said? Presumably he would have said that if your only object is to produce a captain and a cabin boy for the purpose of transferring you from Liverpool to New York, or to manoeuvre a fleet and carry powder from the magazine to the gun, then you need give no more than a shilling to the cabin boy for every pound you give to the more expensively trained captain. But if in addition to this you desire to allow the two human souls which are inseparable from the captain and the cabin boy and which alone differentiate them from the donkey-engine, to develop all their possibilities, then you may find the cabin boy costing rather more than the captain, because the cabin boy's work does not do so much for the soul as captain's work. Consequently you will have to give him at least as much as the captain unless you definitely wish him to be a lower creature, in which case the sooner you are hanged as an abortionist the better.'

It was this insight which gave rise to the efforts which we made to foster a movement to industrial democracy. Partly this turned around the question of human development in industry, and rejected the notion that the division of labour fostered the ultimate wisdom in the wealth of nations. It will be recalled that Adam Smith described the manufacture of pins.

The opening pages of *The Wealth of Nations* contain a careful description

'of the trade of the pin-maker; a workman not educated to this business (which the division of labour has rendered a distinct trade) nor acquainted with the use of the machinery employed in it (to the invention of which the same division of labour has probably given occasion), could scarce, perhaps, with his utmost industry, make one pin in a day, and certainly could not make twenty. But in the way in which this business is now carried on, not only the whole work is a peculiar trade, but it is divided into a number of branches, of which the greater part are likewise peculiar trades. One man draws out the wire, another straights it, a third cuts it, a fourth points it, a fifth grinds it at the top for receiving the head; to make the head requires two or three distinct operations; to put it on is a peculiar business, to whiten the pins is another; it is even a trade by itself to put them into the paper; and the important business of making a pin is, in this manner, divided into about eighteen distinct operations, which, in some manufactories, are all performed by distinct hands, though in others the same man will sometimes perform two or three of them. I have seen a small manufactory of this kind where ten men only were employed, and where some of them consequently performed two or three distinct operations. But though they were very poor, and therefore but indifferently accommodated with the necessary machinery, they could, when they exerted themselves, make among them about twelve pounds of pins in a day. There are in a pound upwards of four thousands pins of a middling size. Those ten persons, therefore, could make among them upwards of forty-eight thousand pins in a day. Each person, therefore, making a tenth part of forty-eight thousands pins, might be considered as making four thousand eight hundred pins in a day. But if they had all wrought separately and independently, and without any of them having been educated to this peculiar business, they certainly could not each of them have made twenty, perhaps not one pin in a day; that is, certainly, not the two hundred and fortieth, perhaps not the four thousand eight hundredth part of what they are at present capable of performing, in consequence of a proper division and combination of their different operations ...

This great increase of the quantity of work which, in consequence of the division of labour, the same number of people are capable of performing, is owing to three different circumstances; first, to the increase of dexterity in every particular workman; secondly, to the saving of the time which is commonly lost in passing from one species of work to another; and lastly, to the invention of a great number of machines which facilitate and abridge labour, and enable one man to do the work of many.' (Adam Smith: *The Wealth of Nations*, Volume One, publisher: J. M. Dent & Sons)

Adam Smith was not insensitive to the conditions which were endured by his pin-makers, but it took a much later analyst, John Ruskin, explicitly to tell us about the true implications of this condition.

'We have much studied and perfected, of late, the great civilised invention of the division of labour; only we give it a false name. It is not, truly speaking, the labour that is divided; but the men: divided into mere segments of men – broken into small fragments and crumbs of life; so that all the little piece of intelligence that is left in a man is not enough to make a pin, or a nail, but exhausts itself in making the point of a pin, or the head of a nail. Now it is a good and desirable thing, truly, to make many pins in a day; but if we could only see with what crystal sand their points were polished – sand of human soul, much to be magnified before it can be discerned for what it is – we should think there might be some loss in it also. And the great cry that rises from all our manufacturing cities, louder than the furnace blast, is all in very deed for this – that we manufacture everything there except men; we blanch cotton, and strengthen steel, and refine sugar, and shape pottery; but to brighten, to strengthen, to refine or to form a single living spirit, never enters into our estimate of advantages.' (Ruskin: *The Stones of Venice*, Section II, chapter vi.)

In the 1960s and '70s, notwithstanding the advance of technology, this admonition remained tellingly relevant. Things have indeed changed, but the crude division of labour still prevails over large parts of the globe, computers notwithstanding. An American scholar, writing in the 1980s, reported that car workers required greatly more skill to drive themselves to work than they did to perform their tasks on the assembly line. Of course, it was not simply the extension of repetitive drudgery that gave rise to the complaint that wage labour was 'wage slavery'. The essential component of that condition was the subordination of one man's will to another.

It was this insight which moved G. D. H. Cole to complain that there were two evils arising from modern capitalism, the least of which was poverty and the greater slavery.

In 1965 I was involved in convening the first seminar on this problem since the gradual forgetting of the messages of the guild socialists, the syndicalists, and other proponents of industrial democracy. This seminar, held in the Adult Education Department of Nottingham University, brought together trade union activists, politicians from various Parties, and a number of academics, mainly working in the field of Adult Education. It was followed by a string of other seminars, which were able to preoccupy themselves with greater and greater attention to the problems in specific industries. These meetings became a regular forum on Workers' Control, and promoted a wide variety of publications.

The adult educationalists included senior members of the profession like Michael Barratt Brown, Tony Topham and a number of others. Their significance was that the current orthodoxy in the teaching of adults was an attempt to apply Socratic methods of teaching. Since adult students were all persons of considerable experience, and since the trade union students, in particular, were practised in a range of skills involving them in negotiations and the organisation of their working colleagues, a consensus had arisen that the delivery of set-piece lectures was likely to be a counterproductive form of tuition. Some of the older Socialist groups were sinners in this respect.

The Socialist Labour League, for instance, was giving 'classes' on Marxism to car workers, in which the lecturer, a doughty Scot from Glasgow, veteran of factional battles reaching back to antiquity, reeled off all the actual examples from volume one of *Capital*, learned by rote. John Daniels senior, who sat through some of these lectures, and knew a few things about pedagogy himself, described this teaching method as 'Shit against the wall. You throw a lot and perhaps a little bit will stick.' The IWC's pedagogues sought to engage the working groups in which they involved themselves in developing their own schemes for democratising their workplaces. In this they were following the example of a previous generation of trade union militants.

In 1968 they resulted in the formation of the Institute for Workers' Control, which had major trade union support, and promoted conferences with the President of the Engineers' Union, Hugh Scanlon, and prominent leaders of the Transport Workers. The seminars, which had begun with fewer than a hundred participants, became major conferences of more than a thousand people.

A major area of concern was the administration of nationalised industries, and other public bodies. Various participatory arrangements had been considered in framing the constitutions of different public enterprises. But overall it was considered that there was too little difference between the status of workers in the public sector and their conditions in private companies. Various proposals had been drawn up, for instance by mineworkers, in the teens and twenties of the last century. These were lovingly disinterred and gave rise to complex proposals for the reform of the National Coal Board.

An extensive discussion took place among steel workers about the administration of their industry after it was renationalised. There were proposals for the democratic administration of the docks, the buses and other concerns. And there were detailed proposals of the extension of trade union powers in the private sector to foster accountability, job security and democratic involvement. Some part of this literature remains in print, and there is a case for reprinting more of it.

The British discussion was overtaken by proposals in Europe for the reform of company law, which gave rise to a public enquiry in Britain under the chairmanship of Lord Bullock. The findings of this investigation were kicked into touch by the Labour Government, after a short but embarrassing hiatus. Mrs. Thatcher was soon to put a stop to other official explorations of these subversive issues.

SONGS

of

INNOCENCE

and of

EXPERIENCE

Shewing the Two Contrary States
of the Human Soul

A Political Life

*Ken Coates
interviewed by
George Lambie*

Dr Lambie is the author of
The Cuban Revolution in
the 21st Century *(Pluto
Press). He interviewed
Ken Coates on several
occasions during the last
months of his life in
connection with research
into political and
economic developments
during the 1970s, from
which these extracts are
taken. Conversation
ranged widely, and we
have selected four themes.
The recordings were
transcribed by Abi Rhodes
and edited by Ken Fleet.*

I

Ken Coates: Tony Benn embarked on a different trajectory from that of Anthony Crosland. He wrote a Fabian pamphlet [relating to industrial democracy] and it was not, in our opinion, very clever. But it represented movement in the right direction, and then, out of the blue, fell the Upper Clyde Shipbuilders (UCS) work-in, and he went and put himself in front of it. From then on it all galloped away and that's when the Council of the Institute for Workers' Control were persuaded to meet him.

George Lambie: It was 1970?

Coates: 1970, something like that. They were all very agnostic about it. They thought this was a sharp Labour politician. That he was just like all the others and that we shouldn't waste much time with him, but gradually he won them over and we invited him to IWC conferences where the rank and file were equally hostile. He went into the lion's den and won approval.

We were excited about alienation because it addressed the fact that people had been totally disempowered and that even with full employment they were not fulfilled. This was not the future that we were labouring for. The human potential had been stopped. Blocked. It was no part of the scheme, and that is what we managed to communicate to Tony Benn, so he got the message, albeit briefly, that we were trying to connect. Not simply that workers' control is about the workers taking all of the decisions; it is about the environment being such that human development is the crucial datum and not profit and loss. That was not Crosland's position.

*   *   *

We had the referendum [in 1974] – the thing that is burned in my memory – we had the referendum and we lost it. We had all been campaigning against the Common Market.

Lambie: This is the referendum on Europe?

Coates: On Europe, yes. We had all been campaigning against the decision to join the Common Market and I went down to see Tony for the 'kitchen cabinet' that we had. I was there early and we were chatting informally. I said, 'I wonder, don't you think that now we have got to prepare contingency plans for what we think must be done at the level of Europe? Since we have lost this argument and are not going to be able to reconnect with it.' Because Stuart Holland, as you know, spent a lot of time trying to actualise what they call the Delors model. He was actually beginning, at the time of this referendum, *Out of Crisis [A Project for European Recovery]*. You know about this?

Lambie: Yes. He sent me the book.

Coates: *Out of Crisis* was a conflab of leftist economists across Europe. Tony Benn was not very smitten with it and he never really embraced it. He wouldn't attack it but he wanted to get on with the real business, which was seizing the commanding heights of power and influence in Britain. Now this is the difficulty with a number of actors when they have all got different goals, and the goals they have are not necessarily the ones that they proclaim. It is not that they are fibbing; it is that they have marked out their spaces and they've developed their political model within the space that they have marked out. That is how I see it. The deputy leadership was lost in 1981 and from then on the Left was on a downward trajectory.

Lambie: You see, from my point of view, but I don't know how accurate this is, because I'm looking at it from an ahistorical position, in some ways, by 1981, it was impossible to implement an Alternative Economic Strategy because the game was off: basically, the markets were wide open and capital controls had been abandoned.

Coates: Yes. I think that is right, but you see the Left couldn't wrap up just because that was the case – you had to have a flag to put up even if it was a rather negative, refusing flag. It should have been put up but we didn't even do that.

Lambie: And that is where Stuart Holland's argument comes in. You had to appeal to European unity as Mitterrand and other leaders were starting to feel the cold winds of free capital movement and losing control at national level.

Coates: I was absolutely with Stuart on that and we tried to do that, which was why I got into the European Parliament. I carried Stuart's proposals through the Parliament. There were a number of lessons that nobody wanted to look at because Delors was also defeated and rejected; it was a forgotten episode. I thought through what we were doing and I was forced to look at the Christian Democrats as a phenomenon we didn't have in England. I started to go to their seminars – they celebrated the centenary of *Rerum Novarum [Papal Encyclical on Capital and Labour, 1891]* – so I began discussions with them. As a result I made this proposal to Delors that we should set up an Assize in which we ask the churches to interrogate civil society about how to implement the full employment programme in Europe. It is really rather important because Delors bought it. I sold him this idea and it enabled me to write to all the church leaders, the Bishops, in Europe – the Protestant Bishops and the Catholic Bishops – and I got them all together to meet on the agenda of the Delors' full employment programme. It was fascinating. The Catholic Bishops sent all these people from the Irish Church, the Jesuits, who were some sort of Latin American Marxists – I found it absolutely riveting. Anyway, we held these great big meetings in the European Parliament, in the President's office, and we had combined meetings of Catholics and Protestants. We didn't get to the Assize because the election took place and I had to push forward to take the rapporteurship on the Parliament's Temporary Committee on Employment that was set up to carry this through the official machine. So I didn't have time to follow all this through. But they followed it through! I had conferences of Jesuits all over the place. They came to Strasbourg and I found that I was at meeting after meeting talking to Jesuits and, of course, it spilled over into the Christian Democracy – that is why we carried Stuart's programme with a virtually 100% majority, because the Christian Democrats had a mandate from a higher authority!

I gave you that pamphlet *[An Assize on Unemployment]*. That has got the politics of it in a nutshell. It's not a very weighty work, but a hell of a lot of work went into that and it showed something that, if the will had existed in the European Commission, there was a tremendous public groundswell in support of a full employment policy for Europe.

Lambie: What year was it that this discussion was taking place?

Coates: 1992-3-4. Getting all those clerics together clearly didn't accomplish much intellectually because they weren't capable of working out a strategy for a viable modern full employment policy in Europe. They had a very developed wish to succeed in this endeavour. There was an awful lot of highly intelligent people in and around the Temporary Committee on Employment who had professional interests at stake and they didn't make a fraction of the progress that the clerics made.

Lambie: So if the church had been behind this it would have acted as a kind of fellow traveller?

Coates: They were behind it, which is why the Christian Democrats all voted in favour of Stuart's documents.

Lambie: These are incredible developments. They could have diverted the course of history to avoid the misery we have today. Has anyone written on this?

Coates: No. I don't think so. You see what happened was that we were ambushed. We carried this through two reports in the Parliament – the second one wasn't quite as unanimous at the first, but it was a bone-crushing majority in each case. The Parliament's reports were not implemented by the Commission.

Lambie: It would be brilliant to set up a research programme on all this, the things you were involved in with Stuart Holland and Tony Benn, because it has been curiously neglected. Some of the people who were at the conference [on the 1970s, held at the British Academy in 2010] even suggested that a lot of the Labour Party documentation from the 1970s has just disappeared. They can't find it anymore; it has been lost.

The thing that was most disappointing about the conference was that there was no sense at all that the 1970s had within it the seed of a possible process of change in which the forces of global capitalism could have been challenged. There was no sense whatsoever that it was a transformative period, which I found quite disappointing. I hold that the 70s were very important in this respect.

I wonder if you would mind if I asked you some specific questions about the Alternative Economic Strategy?

Stuart Holland's line on this, if I have got it correct, is that Labour's Programme 1973 was a pre-cursor to the Alternative Economic Strategy. Stuart made a significant contribution to this document, which he got through a number of committees – Crosland even attended a few of these. Stuart argued that to challenge the forces of globalising business, which was especially powerful in the UK (as articulated in his work, *The Socialist Challenge*) it would be necessary to establish stronger co-operation between the state and business on similar lines to the Italian state holding company [*Instituto per la Riconstruzione Industriale* (IRI)]. On his recommendation, a Trade and Industry sub-committee made a visit to Italy to have a look at how this system operated and came back with an enthusiastic report, of which elements found their way into Labour's Programme. Stuart believed such a strategy might have been acceptable to the revisionists. In fact, Crosland wasn't against this because it accorded with his idea of allowing business and the state to co-operate in a productive way, rather than nationalise 25 big firms or some similar proposal, which became identified later with the Alternative Economic Strategy. It was the noise of nationalisation that was picked up by the right wing press and used to the detriment of the Labour Party, and also frightened people like Crosland and the Right in the Party. So Stuart's view was that using this state/big business model, one could then establish under this umbrella more radical elements of Social Democracy. Stuart gave me a copy of Labour's Programme '73. I read it and, even though I am on the Left, I thought 'my god, this is unbelievable! I think Fidel Castro would have difficulty getting this through in Cuba'. It was an astonishing document and demonstrates just how far politics has moved since then.

Stuart's view is there wasn't an 'alternative economic strategy' at that time, really, it was just Labour's Programme.

Coates: Normally that is right. The Alternative Economic Strategy begins as a project from Cambridge rebels and they sent us a pamphlet and we published it.

They sent it to me and I printed it. I got it supported by the IWC council, which still existed in those days, and so when Tony Benn came to IWC conferences he would find quite a substantial number of people who were thinking about it. Stuart is in the same category – it doesn't diminish Stuart's input in my mind that they came up with those words and outlined that programme.

Lambie: They were the first people to use those words?

Coates: I think so.

Lambie: As I understand it, correct me if I am wrong, first there was Labour's Programme '73, which is a wonderful skeleton for the whole thing, and then the Cambridge pamphlet in which a group of economists at Cambridge added their radical perspective on the implementation of such a programme. When you sent it to me and I first read it I nearly jumped out of my skin because it was extraordinary what they were suggesting; liquidating Britain's assets abroad; placing restraints on the City and a whole series of measures that would basically disengage Britain from the international system. Is it true that IWC members, including yourself, suggested import controls?

Coates: I never suggested an import control in all my life! Our view on these deep policy matters was that people made up the policies that they needed and if they needed import controls they would no doubt say so, and there would be people with their backs to the wall who desperately needed import controls. In the automobile industry, if they are going to shut you down, you might well look with favour on appropriate import controls, but we didn't see it as a matter of principle that there should or shouldn't be import controls – that was perhaps narrow minded – but we were in the position of encouraging groups of workers to make their own demands. Their demands didn't have to be right or wrong, they had to be articulated in a way that would enable people to form a judgement on them, and if there was going to be an argy-bargy about the import controls it would follow at that first stage.

Lambie: OK, so that was the IWC's position?

Coates: That is my position. The IWC was Kilkenny cats – there was a plethora of positions.

Lambie: When we were at the conference in London, Douglas Wass, the Permanent Secretary to the Treasury at that time, said that Tony Benn had been to see him on several occasions but a coherent programme for the

AES was never put forward. Does that make any sense at all?

Coates: Yes, that's right, there wasn't a coherent programme. It didn't make any difference whether Tony spoke with enthusiasm about nationalisation or not, the enemy had got its strategy worked out and they were going to damn it as a programme of nationalising every last sweet shop.

Lambie: I am sure that the forces it was up against were enormous. It is important for me to understand how the AES developed and how the Cambridge group fed into it.

Coates: Yes, but you see it spread out and drew to itself all similar movements past, present and future.

Lambie: So once it was established as the Alternative Economic Strategy it started to gather all kinds of suggestions coming from various groups on the Left, and building up a momentum.

Coates: Yes, and, because it is movable feast, there is no internal consistency in it – the consistency was that we were fed up with what we had got. They needed an alternative but they were pretty open-minded to the point of promiscuity about what would do as an alternative. Nobody had to sit down to start with and define the alternative.

Lambie: So there was an understanding that social democracy was under threat and that something had to be done, and this involved going down a radical path that would strengthen the controls over national level decision making. At the same time the more advanced thinking would involve an element of workers' democracy that would give it legitimacy as a genuine socialist programme.

It seems to me that the forces that were weighed against this were pretty formidable. First of all within the Party itself – Wilson was already shaky about it – a slender majority, the increasingly powerful Right in the Tory Party that was getting support from many quarters: the Treasury, the United States and so on. There is evidence of links between these groups. Then, by the time Callaghan became Prime Minister, it seemed that any strategy for radical change was out of the question.

Coates: There is a lot of information about Callaghan going to MI5 to gather more information about communists in the unions and the origins of the unions' views of these matters. Now the spooks say that they didn't want to get involved in doing Callaghan's inner-party dirty work for him, and that they argued that this was not a function for the security services unless it directly impinged on national security.

I don't know what is true and what is not. I habitually believe that these people get it usually wrong, but perhaps I am mistaken.

Lambie: Tony Benn loses his job as Minister of Industry and becomes the Minster for Energy, weakening support for the AES within the Government, the Cabinet.

Coates: It weakened the experiments in workers' co-ops, but they were going to be stopped anyway, even if Tony had stayed in office. Tony must have been privately relieved that he was shuffled sideways because he wouldn't have to administer the killer punch himself, but they were going under.

I always thought that the workers' co-ops were a bit starry eyed, but I was very pleased that somebody had done it because it got everybody raising their sights and, having said that, it was very obvious that most of them were not going to survive in the marketplace and you couldn't reinvent marketplaces to suit so that many of these were going under. That was my view of it. Whilst they were alive we did what we could to keep them alive and to spread the message. I went all over the country preaching support for them but I think, if Tony Benn hadn't been sacked, there would have been some cathartic moments.

The area where there was a substantial workers' control movement in industry was in the mines. Tony called a conference of the NUM to decide on workers' control and it was fixed. First of all, I wasn't invited and none of the IWC people were invited, although we had published reams and reams of stuff about workers' control in the mines. The miners were all invited, it is true, but they were all very much under control. Peter Heathfield was a workers' control advocate, Jack Dunn was a workers' control advocate from Kent, and there were a number of others, but the conference took place without co-ordination of those people – we didn't know about it, we didn't have prior information about it. Arthur Scargill did have prior information about it, and came with arguments which I could trace back for 50 years to previous debates within the miners' union when changes of status were being discussed. Arthur argued that you couldn't have workers' control because it would be divided authority, that you had to have a single fountain of authority so that there had to be a Coal Board as the unilateral authority and the Union as the unilateral opposition. It would be too confusing to mix their roles. That was his very stupid argument and why Tony bought it I don't know.

Tony as Secretary of State for Energy was, from an early stage, switched off from the argument for industrial democracy in the one place where it could have had electric results. You just think, if the miners had got a veto over hiring and firing decisions – that is elementary workers' control. The dockers had practised it for years on end. If they had got that, what would have happened to the miners' strike? I'll tell you what would have happened to it; it wouldn't have happened because there would have been nothing to strike about. They would have to get rid of the miners' self-government rights before they could introduce the measures that created the strike. That is, of course, why Arthur wasn't keen on giving them these powers, because that would make it more difficult to get his strike, and his model of socialist advance was 'everybody out on strike, Thatcher overthrown, red flag flies, glory, glory hallelujah!'

Many, many things have happened and they are not all bad. Tony fell in with Arthur on the miners' strike. By and large it required a lot of courage and it required a lot of dedication – as a strategy it was not very clever. It was pretty much bound to finish the way it did with the government putting the resources it put and with the unions possessing the resources they possessed. I'll give you an example: Tony came and he sat in the same chair you are in now on the day that he had decided that he was going to make an appeal to all the workers in England to come out in support of the miners – it was in December that year – and he said, 'I think we have got now to cast discretion to the winds and we have got to call on them all to stop the miners from being defeated'. Well, I couldn't believe my ears. I said, 'when you issue this call, Tony, who do you think is going to come? Because you can, in two minutes, lift people's hearts by calling for an audacious move, but what happens when nobody accepts the invitation?' And I knew nobody was going to accept the invitation because I wasn't in Westminster, I was actually teaching trade union classes in Derby and I had remembered so well what had happened when the miners' strike broke out. There was a huge flush of enthusiasm and my shop stewards all saw this – shops stewards from three foundries – and they were full of enthusiasm about what was happening, and how they took a collection for the miners and everybody was chucking in their five pound notes. It really was a moment of enormous exhilaration. Three weeks into the strike it all went topsy-turvy and what happened was the flying pickets came down –

and a boy was killed with a thrown rock. He was a picket, but it didn't make any difference; in the press there was now a huge campaign against the violence and it wasn't that the stewards turned against the strike – they didn't – but they described to me what they were doing. 'Now we have to take the collection privately. If we simply put the bucket in a place people would walk past it. They don't want to be seen contributing. If you go up to them privately and say are you going to give us a quid for the miners, they'll do it.' It did become a suspect activity. That was right at the beginning of the procedure and so, when Tony is going to call on the whole working class to come out, it was a no-no. There was nothing possible in that stratagem. You know where he got it from? He got it from Arthur.

I tried to persuade Tony that this was not the best contribution he could make, but he went and did it. He havered when he was talking to me but he went straight out and made the broadcast. We turned the wireless on and there it was – 'don't sit and watch it on television, come out and help us'. Instead of coming to help us, even more miners went back to work. That is a failure in generalship. I don't blame Tony very much for this because it is a failure in generalship of Arthur Scargill who, as the leader of the strikers, is supposed to know what his men want to do and can take. Tony was the leader of the Labour Movement and it was not his finest moment. If that had been the sum total of our relationship it would have come to an end, but it wasn't because of a lot of other things that we were doing.

The miners' strike was a trauma. It wouldn't have happened if Tony had gone with us on workers' control when the mining structures were being considered. If we had a classic workers' control regime in which the miners controlled hiring and firing, and in which nobody could be dismissed or downgraded without the approval of the workforce, then it would certainly have been an obstacle to Thatcher's procedures. Yes, she could have got over it, she could have annulled Tony Benn's Labour legislation, but then that would have been a rumpus that might have very well produced a universal miners' strike instead of a partial one. So, who is to say that might not have won? In any case, there are too many ifs and too many buts, and that is why I am not in the mood to foam at the mouth when I think of the mistakes that Tony made. But I think they were mistakes.

Lambie: What would you say was the greatest obstacle to implementing the Alternative Economic Strategy?

Coates: You have to have people who want it. You needed a socialist movement that believed in itself. The last time that looked anything like real in Britain was in the period we were talking about when, possibly, Crosland, Benn and the other disparate group of people could, if they had seen eye-to-eye, have sold an alternative perspective. Even then there would have been a number of important people with strategic positions in the Labour Movement who would have died in the last ditch to stop them, such as Ray Gunter and George Brown, all kinds of people.

Lambie: Do you think there was a special moment, at the time of the IMF crisis [in 1976], when it might have been possible that Labour's Programme/the AES, could have been put in place if there had been a rejection of the International Monetary Fund's demands?

Coates: I can't say it isn't possible, but by the time that the IMF settlement had been reached I think that the game was up.

Lambie: I agree with that entirely. I looked at some of the cabinet minutes which showed that Tony Benn sought to promote what was essentially the Alternative Economic Strategy as an alternative to accepting the controls of private capital.

Coates: Yes, but he wasn't carrying …

Lambie: No. True. But had Crosland, who was disenchanted by the demands of the IMF and said some quite interesting things – 'we have to stop paying Danegeld' etc – had Crosland sided with Tony Benn, he and his followers wouldn't have had anything to put in place, yet the Left did have a plan in the form of the AES which contained a strategy for challenging the powers of private capital that were controlling the situation. Rejection might have precipitated the scenario envisaged by the Cambridge group in which Britain would have been almost forced to consider the possibility of going it alone.

Coates: I doubt very much whether you can get that kind of agreement: you can't make a silk purse out of a pig's ear. Which heroes were going to stand up and die in the last ditch for going it alone. In the event even Tony Benn didn't die in the last ditch; certainly Crosland didn't.

Lambie: I think this is the biggest problem and Tony Benn identifies this as well. There was potentially a programme in place that could have diverted Britain down another route, and it says in the document by the

Cambridge Group that, if a major power – and Britain was most important in this respect – could disengage itself from the international system, this would disrupt the forces of global capital that were gaining strength at that time. I think that is true, but, as you say, the problem lies with the fact that there just simply wasn't the political will or understanding of the situation; it might have been right at the time but it couldn't have been implemented because there weren't the personalities or the politics to carry it through.

Coates: How would you mobilise? All this was an argument going on in the Cabinet. Even the closest followers didn't know the circumstances of what was being agreed and the likely consequences of their implementation. There was no broad debate – a little bit of a debate happened afterwards but that was all 'who'd have thought it'. I think that by the time we got there it was too late and I don't think it made any difference whether Tony Benn was Secretary of State for Industry or Secretary of State for Energy. He had a good run whilst he was Secretary of State for Energy and for Industry, but essentially this was to do with a loss of confidence by Wilson. Wilson didn't know whether he could get away with disciplining Benn and whether there would be a rumpus that would be too costly, and by the time that he moved him he did know that Varley would do as he was told and that Benn would not be able to resist. It was the fact that he moved Benn that was the mortal blow, that Benn was incapable of preventing this sideways shuffle.

Lambie: One of the things the Europeans perhaps felt was that acquiescence to the International Monetary Fund signalled a British left-leaning Labour Government had given way to external forces that demanded a change of sovereign policies to comply with what were ultimately the interests of private capital. I think European Governments were scared of this because they felt 'when is our turn coming' even though their economies were much more closed, much more controlled and they had kicked out a lot of the Eurodollar market activity from their own economies in the early 1970s. Much of this is hypothetical. I think, ultimately, we all agree, that there just simply wasn't the political support, the momentum, or the interventions that would have been necessary to implement the Alternative Economic Strategy had the government rejected the IMF. There were all sorts of problems. But I do think the moment was interesting historically because, had something like the AES been put in place at that particular time and got European support on co-operative capital controls, it would have been a big event!

Coates: Sure!

Lambie: The Americans were partly reliant on what was happening in London to finance the operations of their multinationals. US Secretary of State William Rogers commented:

> 'We all had the feeling it [the initial attempts to deregulate finance] could come apart in a quite serious way as I saw it, it was a choice between Britain remaining in the liberal financial system of the West as opposed to a radical change of course, because we were concerned about Tony Benn precipitating a decision by Britain to turn its back on the International Monetary Fund. I think if that had happened then the whole system would have come apart – God knows what Italy might have done, then France might have taken a radical change in the same direction. It would not only have had consequences for the economic recovery, it would have had great political consequences, so we tended to see it in cosmic terms.'

What they were worried about was that, if the Labour Left shut down the London financial markets, it would be a real problem because that was where the axis of multinational power was based at that time.

Coates: And that is what actually called the next shots because they got a big scare in that crisis and decided not to have any more of those scares and that is why, subsequently – when Labour was defeated and Thatcher was securely in place – the Americans initiated the British American Project, which was a careful surgical attack on the Labour Left to remove anti-Americanism as a part of the British political firmament.

Lambie: Do you have information on this?

Coates: Lots. They set this up. They put huge amounts of money into this. They set up a network of American and British pundits and regular meetings, expensive seminars and permanent dialogue – one of the key men was Jonathan Powell. He is attached to the Embassy [in Washington] and then he's Blair's manager.

Lambie: Interesting.

Coates: Yes!

Lambie: And they also linked up to the whole 'democracy promotion' programme?

Coates: Yes! And this is why I can afford to be really very permissive about my comrades and realise sometimes all of us are going to make mistakes and we have to pick ourselves up and make the best of things, because you are up against a remorseless adversary in which none of these normal courtesies apply. The British American Project was Blair. They were not going to have a repeat where alternative economic strategies were bobbing out of the woodwork.

Lambie: That is really interesting.

Coates: Where would they come from, these alternative economic strategies? I don't know, it might have come out of Europe.

Lambie: Mitterrand was soon nipped in the bud, wasn't he?

Coates: In Europe we did a little revolution. When I was elected [to the European Parliament, in 1989] with a handful of other so-called pro-Europeans, we made a *coup d'état* in the British Labour Group. It was called 'British Labour Group' because that was the name given to County Council associations of councillors for their factional meetings, and so I put down a motion changing the name of the British Labour Group to the 'European Parliamentary Labour Party' (EPLP), which did two things at the same time. On the one hand, it ended the association with local government, which was downgrading the whole show; on the other, it claimed an element of parity with the Parliamentary Labour Party. Just as the Parliamentary Labour Party had claimed that it couldn't be instructed what to do by the Party *hoi polloi* because it represented the voters of the whole country, so the European Parliamentary Labour Party represented the voters of the whole country and so couldn't be ordered about by the party hierarchy. Well, they did a counter-revolution. They didn't change the constitution but they sacked everybody. They cut down the size of the EPLP from 60 odd to, I think, 13, by getting them all defeated. But there had been a potential for some kind of opposition. It took Blair to make that counter-revolution. It was organised by Mandelson.

In a way the Delors programme [of 1993 and later] was a continuation, precisely at the European level, of what we were trying to do earlier. From my perspective it was a very worthwhile struggle because it was too late in the day by the 1980s, the early '90s, to do a unilateral declaration of independence by one country. It would have been impossible because that country would have been smashed. But to have had a European-wide response to the problems that were already being created by the free markets and globalisation would have been very viable.

*   *   *

Lambie: Is Jack Jones still alive?

Coates: No. He died in 2009.

Lambie: Last year? I seem to remember something about him.

Coates: He was a great man, Jack Jones. He always supported us when we raised questions about Soviet dissidents and he also gave a prodigious amount of support to the idea of workers' control. He gave me powerful encouragement because I was in a lot of trouble in those days. I was on the wrong side of Harold Wilson.

It was the Vietnam War. I was opposed to the Vietnam War and I got expelled from the Labour Party. I fought a four-year battle to be reinstated and I was reinstated and Harold Wilson did not like it. Because, after I had been expelled, I wrote a pamphlet against Wilson's support for the Americans in Vietnam. There is a revisionist school of history that says Wilson never really supported the Americans; but he did, he didn't send troops because that would have cooked his goose. Wilson went down the line of least resistance and I wrote a pamphlet that was a bit rude. I went to town on him and there was one *bon mot* of which I was particularly proud, which was, for Harold Wilson, 'a straight line is the shortest breach between two promises'. It was noted in Transport House; Sarah Barker who was in charge of the internal secret police of the Labour Party made a note of all these things. The Institute for Workers' Control in the meantime gathered a lot of support, including support from all the main unions, and so when my appeal came up Ron Hayward was the General Secretary, and the union leaders were now cracking the whip on the Executive – there was Jack and Hugh Scanlon – and it was decided that I was going to be reinstated. So, there was a ceremonial meeting of the National Executive and Sarah Barker – the proposal was that I should be reinstated, which got the support of Ron Hayward and the union leaders and all the rest of them, it was more or less a formality, it was bound to happen – and Sarah Barker came to the bar – in those days she couldn't sit in the Executive, it is not like that now – but she came and stood and read her speech to the National Executive and the reason she wanted to speak was that she wanted to say that they shouldn't reinstate me because of all the outrageous and blasphemous things that I said about our Prime Minister, Mr Wilson. Then she proceeded to read them all out and they all got the giggles because I was actually fairly candid about him and I hit the target. They were all pissed off with him because he was trying to bring in 'In Place of Strife' and this and that, so they were all squirming with laughter and, anyway, they heard her out and then they reinstated me. Later, I was very sorry for Harold Wilson because he got Alzheimer's.

They did reinstate me, but the second time they expelled me I didn't ask them to reinstate me.

Lambie: The second time they expelled you; what date was that?

Coates: 1997/8. It was when Blair had taken over and I had published a booklet about Clause Four, in defence of Clause Four. Of course, Clause Four included the best available system of democratic control and that had been our saving grace in the Labour Party that we could actually appeal to Clause Four. We were vigorously opposed to all of the managerial suppositions that went into nationalisation, but, none the less, when Blair came to rubbish it, I wrote this booklet [*Common Ownership*] to defend Clause Four and I was in the firing line with Blair.

Blair came out to Brussels to read the riot act because more than half of the European Parliamentary Labour Party signed an appeal that I had drafted in favour of Clause Four. They put it as an advert in *The Guardian* on the day that he was due to come on a fundraiser: he was furious. Anyway, it was clear to me about the annulment of Clause Four. The document they came to propose was rubbish. The authors of Clause Four, Sidney and Beatrice Webb, were not model philosophers but they wrote something which was internally consistent and cogently argued and sustainable. This new Clause Four was total rubbish. It was vapid. It was nothing and it was not intended to be anything. It was intended to get them out of the situation they were in. What they wanted to do was to be able to privatise everything that moved and everything else that couldn't move and get very rich.

*   *   *

II
Cuba

Coates: I don't want to reminisce about Cuba, but I had enormous affection for Che.

Lambie: Did you meet him?

Coates: No. That is what I deeply regret. I met Fidel and talked to him and that was an extraordinary meeting. I went and was debriefed for about a fortnight and Bertrand Russell had a wonderful idea, which was that there should be an international brigade that was to go to Vietnam and he sold it to Sartre and they, jointly, proposed it to Fidel. They sent me to go and get Fidel's answer.

Lambie: That was a nice mission to be on.

Coates: So I went to get it. They kept me for about a fortnight debriefing me to see if we were crackers, to satisfy themselves that really I was representing Russell. In the end, I was taken – told to get up at five o'clock in the morning – and taken in a jeep into the interior and they gave me a set of fatigues because the jeep threw up a tremendous amount of dust. Foul. Filthy. I was with Ralph Schoenman [then Russell's secretary] and the pair of us were taken for hours, nine hours, maybe more, through really rough jungle roads. I can remember an eagle swooping out of the sky and picking up a long snake with its claws and flying away. It was the back of beyond. Finally, our jeep met Fidel's convoy with Fidel in front. He wasn't daft – he didn't drink all the dust! We were then followed by twenty or so jeeps who were on tour with him plotting whatever they had to plot and we just tagged on at the end. We drove for another two or three hours and we found ourselves in the upper mountains where there was a wonderful school perched on top of the mountain and the convoy stopped and Fidel got out of the jeep and welcomed us. It was like a Western film!

Lambie: You might have got as far as Santiago.

Coates: We could have done. It was miles away from anywhere. It was a pre-existing boarding school, which had been taken over by the high command. Anyway, Fidel invited us to go and get washed and meet him for dinner, which we did. Dinner was a long, long haul and they brought in roast pig, roast lamb, and people were invited to help themselves. We sat opposite Fidel with a very wonderful doctor and close advisor of Fidel's. We talked about Russell's wonderful scheme and Fidel said, and this is why I had been kept waiting about for a fortnight, he said he had heard from Ho Chi Minh to the effect that they didn't want an international brigade, and the penny dropped with me at once because I have got a funny kind of mind. Ralph Schoenman was absolutely spare about this, he was bereft, because he did want an international brigade. He was a gung-ho laddie. He was a crazy so and so, but he had some merits as well as a few drawbacks. I could see this. I reasoned like this: if there is an international brigade, what does Ho Chi Minh get from this? He gets a whole bunch of rebellious students from Paris and London who can't fight and are really not much use.

Lambie: If it doesn't have the big media effect then it could be a liability to him.

Coates: That was the least of the problems. What does he do if he has got all these deadbeats trying to learn to engage the enemy in battle and ten thousand Russians and twenty thousand Chinese? And, if he allows them in, how does he get rid of them?

Lambie: Yes, exactly.

Coates: It seemed to me that that was the operative question. I have got the wrong sort of mind for this. Ralph was an innocent and he wanted to help the Vietnamese, but I thought it might not help the Vietnamese too much. This conversation lasted all night. It didn't start until a little while before midnight and it didn't finish until nearly six o'clock in the morning and it was a riveting conversation, but not the one we'd expected. We followed Fidel around the next morning. We were going to look at strawberry farms that morning. He was getting strawberries for his ice-cream parlour. He had opened a huge ice-cream parlour in central Havana, which was to have as big a variety of ice-creams as the Americans had got – this was very important, so we had to go and look at strawberries. There was a huge territory which was in a plain, that was now strawberry farms and we went to investigate them. We also called in on some peasants in the hills on the way down – really dirt poor peasants – and I remember in their dwellings they had got cast aluminium statues, one was of the Virgin Mary and one was of Fidel and they were hanging there on the wall. Anyway, we followed them around and Ralph had a bit of a fit about them not getting Ho Chi Minh's agreement, and he wanted Fidel to wait until he, Ralph, had gone back to see Ho Chi Minh and persuaded him otherwise.

Lambie: And by that time Fidel would have had immense international cachet on the Left. Ho Chi Minh, the communication would have been very solid between those two?

Coates: Yes. They knew what they were talking about. That's why they kept me waiting a fortnight.

Lambie: While they thought it through?

Coates: While they thought it through, yes. I think they were right. Bertie would have allowed himself to be persuaded by Ralph if there was any chance that it was going to happen; but he was very cross with the Americans and wanted the Vietnamese to win. The subsequent story – Fidel said to us 'we can't do that but why don't you help us with a project in Latin America?' It hadn't been announced at that time and we didn't know what it was, but it was Che Guevara in Bolivia. That was an ill-fated project.

*   *   *

III
European Nuclear Disarmament

Coates: Stuart Holland came into my life through the Institute for Workers' Control, which he found interesting. He did what he could and he continued working with his European connections to create *Out of Crisis*. I was not centrally involved in that but I was peripherally involved. I gave it what support I could, which was quite a lot. We published the book and I attended some of the meetings. Stuart went on to advise Willy Brandt with Jan Pronk on the creation of the Brandt Report. During this time I was involved in and happy to create European Nuclear Disarmament, which we set up with Edward Thompson, but there were two different views about what it should be. The idea was that since we now had the threat of Euro missiles, the installation of Cruise missiles and Pershing missiles all across Europe, that the unilateral perspective, which was suitable for British nuclear disarmament, was no longer adequate. Which is not a repudiation of unilateralism in Britain, but it is actually an affirmation that you have to create a European perspective; many of the European countries didn't have nuclear weapons, those that housed nuclear weapons were hosting other people's – mostly American. The east European countries were housing Russian missiles. So, we invented this idea of removing all the nuclear weapons from the continent of Europe, from Poland to Portugal, and to create a campaign for a nuclear-free-zone in all of Europe. Edward was less keen on the nuclear-free-zone idea because he wanted to concentrate on a popular campaign which would mobilise the masses. He wanted a new CND. At times he erred into almost thinking that you could create a serial unilateralism, but we were able to work out that difference. My view was that we needed to create an inclusive movement of the parties of the Left and Centre, of such churches that would co-operate, of peace movements and the young. Our paths diverged because Edward concentrated on propaganda in England on the margins of CND, talking to the same audience essentially but widening the audience, because a lot of people found it attractive to think in European terms (a lot of young people). I concentrated on trying to get a European movement and we formed a campaign which was bringing together supporters for the appeal of European Nuclear Disarmament from the major west European countries. There were a few east European sympathisers. I didn't see our task as being to concentrate on European nuclear disarmament for the east; I brought all the people who came from the east into this discussion, but they were a handful. There was Roy and Zhores Medvedev in Russia, there were two or three other distinguished dissidents, there was the former Hungarian prime minister András Hegedüs and a group of students around him. I was in correspondence with the pupil of Robert Havemann, a prominent East German dissident communist who was under house arrest. We [Michael Meacher MP and Ken Coates] went to Berlin to see him and it so happened that we went on the day he actually died. There were a number of east Europeans who were endorsing this approach. Edward wanted to build a mass movement of east Europeans and Roy Medvedev said it is impossible, you can't do that. Well, it wasn't impossible, but it wasn't a very peace loving movement we created there, it was a movement of growing dissidents that accompanied the disintegration of communist control in Russia – that is a later story. The main work, that I was doing, was to build up the west European movement, which we did.

Lambie: And your capacity then was as a Euro MP?

Coates: No, I wasn't a Euro MP [then].

Lambie: Not at that stage, no?

Coates: I was an agitator.

Lambie: An agitator. OK. So this is the end of the '80s we are talking about is it? Or early '80s?

Coates: Yes, starting in 1982 we organised a convention in Brussels and we got there, for the first time in one haul, a conference of a thousand odd people including the Social Democrats, and the Labour Party were represented.

Lambie: Where is the peace movement in relation to this?

Coates: Bruce Kent came. Lots of people from the peace movement were there. It was partly their show but there were also the main Social Democratic Parties, most of them just beginning to flirt with this. The Labour Party was in on the organisation – the Spanish Socialists, the Italian Communists, the Spanish Communists all came. There was a substantial political representation; quite a substantial church involvement and the major peace movements, which were not just the British, there was the Dutch IKV [Interchurch Peace Council] as well as the Belgians.

Lambie: Wasn't there the World Peace Council as well?

Coates: Yes, that was not us. That was a communist front organisation. We invited them to come along but I don't think they did at that time. That was the Brussels Convention and it was highly successful. Edward was very cross about it because it was getting a united front of Left parties and in-house organisations as well as the peace movement. We resolved to go to Berlin for the second Convention the following year, which was in 1983.

That was an amazing conference. It was the first time we had all Social Democratic parties, all the Communist parties except one, the Greens en masse – such as they were, Petra Kelly and all the other prominent Greens – plus all the peace movements. There were about 4,000 people at this conference throughout the day. They had some famous spats, the Greens confronted the Social Democrats; they went over into East Berlin and played silly buggers. I had to go and mediate, but it all passed off splendidly.

Lambie: OK. What was the central organising body of all this?

Coates: Us.

Lambie: As?

Coates: As the European Nuclear Disarmament liaison committee, which had been set up for this purpose. I was the secretary. Edward didn't want to go to Berlin. He said it was a provocation against the Russians and we'd be crushed. He said all sorts of things. He just didn't want to be in a movement which had all the Social Democrats and all the Communists kicking into the same goal. I did want to be in that. We got Willy Brandt there, and we got everyone there and I think it was our finest hour. Because they not only went there, they managed to maintain an agreement for European nuclear disarmament – no nuclear weapons in Europe! That was big stuff.

One of the things that was big stuff was that it was fiercely attacked by Yuri Zhukov, the President of the Soviet Peace Committee. He attacked myself and Luciana Castellina [an Italian politician active in END] and a couple of other people by name. Edward was not pleased by that. As it was, Zhukov gave us the imprimatur so I answered Zhukov in some detail, and I answered him in terms of what was to become Perestroika. The thing then went on and we had a third Convention in Perugia, in Italy. A fourth one in Amsterdam. Another one in Paris. Another one in Lund. A lot of them. It was a working movement. As time went on, of course, it began to fall out. These things are inevitable. And the peace movements found that they didn't really get on very well with the Social Democrats or the Communists and the churches wondered whether they were in the right pot. There was a mass of trade union involvement. I think it was a big thing.

Lambie: Was this vehicle seen as having just the purpose of nuclear disarmament?

Coates: Certainly.

Lambie: Or was it also seen as a vehicle for bringing together the Left and the middle ground in politics?

Coates: No. It wasn't.

Lambie: It was just about nuclear disarmament?

Coates: It was about disarming nuclear weapons out of Europe. That is why it could bring all of these others together. It wasn't telling them they had to get together; that was implying criticising them for not being together. It didn't get into any of that.

Lambie: So they could rally around that common cause and that was it?

Coates: That was it, and they were doing it, and they were doing it continuously from one year to the next. And in between times we had a liaison committee which met probably four to six times a year to organise the participation. It had a big impact. All the Greek Left were there; Andreas Papandreou was there. All the Spanish Left were there.

Lambie: Was Stuart Holland involved at that time?

Coates: Yes, he used to come, but he was busy doing other things. He came because it was interesting. That is when I went into the European Parliament. I had decided that it was sensible to see if we could use that platform, which we could. Then Gorbachev came along and 1989 came along and The Wall fell down and the fractiousness of the peace movement began to know no bounds. There were so many things to fall out about and there were a few more that could be invented so that the falling out was rather general. I didn't engage in that. By this time I was in the European Parliament and I had to find a way to carry on the impetus of the nuclear disarmament movement.

Lambie: Let me just ask you, Ken, you are now back in the Labour Party?

Coates: I've been back in the Labour Party for decades.

Lambie: Yes, but you were expelled.

Coates: I was reinstated, I think, in 1969. By this time I was becoming, I'm afraid, something of an establishment in the Labour Party. That is why Kinnock used to think that I was alright – I was alright to represent him in China. I wasn't sure if I wanted to represent him in China. That is a different question. Anyway, that happened in the middle of all this. I took the European Nuclear Disarmament movement to China to involve the Chinese and the Chinese came. The Chinese sent a powerful delegation – a little delegation to Berlin and a big one to Perugia. It had got some momentum and I thought that perhaps the way to carry this thing on in the post-1989 world was to propose to the European Parliament that it should organise a joint session with the Supreme Soviet. They thought I was absolutely crazy, but we carried it through the European Parliament and Gorbachev thought it was a great idea. What we did was to make a common space between two emergent organisations – the European Parliament didn't quite know what its role was and was not set in its ways, and the Supreme Soviet was discovering democracy, somewhat falteringly, but it was, none the less. So, Gorbachev put in a man called Zagladin, who was rather a splendid man. I got on with him famously. He was a cynical old bastard. But anyway, it was his job to organise the joint meeting between the European Parliament and the Supreme Soviet. We were running at it great guns. I had got the Socialist Group of the European Parliament who sent a delegation. The Christian Democrats agreed in principle to the convening of the joint session and it was all on the go. Then Gorbachev was kidnapped and Yeltsin took over and the Supreme Soviet ceased to exist so we couldn't have a joint session with it. Yeltsin wasn't interested in any such thing.

Lambie: You obviously didn't approach him because it wouldn't be worth it?

Coates: No, it was pointless, absolutely pointless. So that is where I think END stopped. END would have carried on if we had had the joint session because we would have had, as it were, a disarmament chapter. Life would have been different. We wouldn't have had the expansion of NATO into the former Warsaw Pact territories and we wouldn't have had the continuation of the Cold War, we would have had a different regime. I think that would have worked, but it didn't work because we got Yeltsin instead and they privatised everything that wasn't screwed to the wall, and the Social Democrats began their inexorable drift into neo-liberalism.

Not a very clever story. We didn't anticipate that, weren't ready for it, didn't know what to do about it. That is the background which I brought to Stuart's attempt to capitalise on Delors' white paper on employment, productivity and whatever the hell it was. Anyway, that is where I came from. The next thing I did was to run an offensive to get the European churches on board for full employment.

*   *   *

IV
Bukharin and China

Coates: I have been working through my reminiscences about the Bukharin case. As you know, I was very much engaged in trying to get Bukharin rehabilitated.

The Bukharin story was an important one. I was a friend of Roy Medvedev [author of *Let History Judge: The Origins and Consequences of Stalinism*] and Roy corresponded with me. He still corresponds with me but then he was regularly sending me things to appeal about and make a fuss about and bang drums on. Then, out of the blue, came a letter from a man called Yuri Larin. Yuri Larin was born Yuri Bukharin and he was a toddler, a baby, when his father was arrested and entered into this nightmare of a trial. Yuri was taken away from his mother and, first of all, put in an orphanage, and then adopted, and he didn't know who his father was. When he was a teenager he found and was ultimately reunited with his mother who had been in the Gulag and was let out when he was about 18. They were together again and he started appealing for the rehabilitation of his dad. He wrote to Khrushchev at about the time when Khrushchev fell, and they were messed about from pillar to post, him and his mother, trying to get this rehabilitation. Finally, he made up his mind after a decade or more to try to get the support of Berlinguer, the Italian Communist leader, because he was thought to be a liberal minded fellow. Well, he was, but he was also a lazy fellow, and he was also preoccupied with things in Italy. He didn't answer Yuri Larin, who wrote him a very moving letter. I was sent the letter by Roy and so I set about manoeuvring a situation in the Italian Communist Party that would get Berlinguer to be more accommodating. I launched a world appeal for the rehabilitation of Bukharin signed by dissident communists and not-so-dissident communists and socialists and all kinds of people. We got a few thousand signatures but in Italy I wrote to the decent old guard of the Socialist Party like Lombardi. They all signed up and caused a nuisance all over the place in the Communist Party. So they signed up, not Berlinguer, but all the important people and the Moscow correspondents and no end of people.

Lambie: When was this Ken, what were the dates?

Coates: 1978. That was the 40th anniversary of the murder of Bukharin. After a serious inquisition Berlinguer asked the Instituto Gramsci to convene a conference on Bukharin and they got Stephen Cohen, who was Bukharin's biographer, and they invited a lot of people. I had to be invited because I caused all this nuisance. I went and it was a fascinating meeting. All the scholars were there, the people you would expect such as Alec Nove and Moshe Lewin, and a lot of very distinguished Sovietologists. But there were also all kinds of other people who were there for political reasons. By far the most important person was Su Shaozhi who was the director of the Institute of Marxism-Leninism-Mao Zedong Thought.

That is when I met Su and I made a beeline for him and I sat up all night with him for three nights. He took my pamphlet on Bukharin and translated it into Chinese and published it in 70,000 copies – I never had so many fond readers – so Bukharin was well and truly rehabilitated in China, albeit quietly. It was important, it was a mixed blessing because Bukharin in China was Bukharin's policy on the peasantry, which had a mixed significance. In any case it doesn't matter, but rehabilitating Bukharin in China meant something very different from rehabilitating him in Russia. In Russia it meant freedom of thought and expression, open debate, and in China it didn't mean that, it meant a different policy towards the countryside. Be that as it may, it opened the door for me and I was invited backwards and forwards to the Institute of Marxism-Leninism-Mao Zedong Thought. That is why I took Stuart Holland to China to sell his Brandt Report to the Chinese Communist Party. We connected this and the Brandt Report became a cause of the Chinese Communists and they went to a great conference on it in Peru, organised by the Socialist International.

I had been to China before I had even met Su. I met Zhou Enlai in 1971 and that was a most extraordinary meeting. I dried up completely. I had never been so overawed by a person as I was by Zhou Enlai. Of course, he had the whole weight of the Mandarinate behind him and he was so extraordinarily well briefed – a powerful man. Normally, I am not terribly impressed by power, but it wasn't just power in his case.

Nobody was allowed into China. How I got into China was a bit of a scheming thing. The Americans gave the go ahead for the overthrow of Sihanouk in Cambodia, and Lon Nol, who was an American puppet, made a *coup d'état.* Sihanouk was voyaging abroad and instead of going back to Phnom Penh he went back to Beijing and started a government in exile. I made contact with Sihanouk and offered moral support from the Russell Foundation. We thought that if Sihanouk could be reinstated this would be the beginning of a series of rebuffs for the CIA. Sihanouk responded and we developed a touching correspondence and, as a result, I was invited by Sihanouk to go to meet him in Beijing. So I had to be given a visa. It became a matter of diplomatic relations between Sihanouk and the Chinese. So, having got the visa, I drafted a proposal for a re-launching of the International Peace Movement for the attention of the Chinese, and that is how I was invited to see Zhou Enlai. It was interesting. He didn't agree because the peace movement, as far as he was concerned, was inseparable from his potty little communist parties, which were all at loggerheads; they were in a state of violent combat. So I can't tell you that this was a resounding success this meeting, although it was a fascinating experience, and it stood me in good stead for years because the Chinese knew I had been to see Zhou Enlai and that opened more doors than you could possibly imagine.

I didn't go back again because there was no point until I met Su Shaozhi, and I went back with END. I tried to create a relationship with the Chinese and the European peace movements, which was the same agenda that I put to Zhou Enlai earlier, but this time we pulled it off. It didn't do us any good, did it? It was a very interesting set of experiences.

COMMUNICATION WORKERS UNION

May Day Greetings

Billy Hayes
General Secretary

Jane Loftus
President

Infant Joy

I have no name
I am but two days old.
What shall I call thee?
I happy am
Joy is my name —
Sweet joy befall thee!

Pretty joy!
Sweet joy but two days old.
Sweet joy I call thee;
Thou dost smile.
I sing the while
Sweet joy befall thee.

The Institute for Workers' Control

Michael Barratt Brown

Michael Barratt Brown is the founding Principal of Northern College.

In the year 2003, Ken Coates collected together and had published a number of articles which he had written in the 1960s and 70s on industrial democracy and entitled the book, *Workers' Control – Another World is Possible.* He obtained contributions from the newly elected leaders of two of the largest unions, Derek Simpson of the Engineers' Union and Tony Woodley of the Transport & General Workers, together with supporting introductory messages from five other unions, the journalists, the firemen, the communications workers, the bakers, and public and commercial services unions. This initiative from Ken was most particularly encouraged by the inaugural speech of Tony Woodley on his election as leader of the T&G, which he spoke of as giving 'A Mandate for Change'. This was in the sixth year of the so-called 'New Labour' Government of Tony Blair, which was committed to the abandonment of many of the principles of the Labour Party; social ownership, industrial democracy, public welfare services, and regulation by the United Nations of international disputes. In welcoming the 'rebirth of the trade union spirit', Tony Woodley had singled out victory in the struggle for industrial democracy, which was yet to come.

The founding of the Institute for Workers' Control (IWC) at the sixth annual conference on Workers' Control, held at Nottingham University in 1968, followed a series of earlier conferences among trade unionists, left-wing Labour Party members, and university lecturers in Industrial Studies, which were initiated by Ken Coates, himself an ex-coal miner and then an extra-mural tutor in adult education at

Nottingham University. The background to this initiative was the return of a Labour Government, in 1964, under Harold Wilson as Premier after thirteen years of Conservative rule, but with a very small majority, somewhat increased at a further election in 1966, but still without the commitment to socialist advance and trade union involvement that many in the Labour Party were looking for. Ken Coates' initiative in founding the Institute really built on a campaign promoted over a number of years by *Voice of the Unions*, a monthly journal sponsored by left-wing MPs and trade unionists. On the initiative of Ernie Roberts, Assistant General Secretary of the Engineers' Union, *Voice of the Unions* had organised two conferences, one in 1964 in Nottingham, which attracted 80 participants, one in London in 1965, with the support of the London Co-operative Society, which had many more participants. A further conference, on 'Opening the Books' of companies to trade union review, was jointly organised, later in 1965, with the Manchester-based paper *Labour's Voice*. A conference in early 1966 in Nottingham, convened by the Centre for Socialist Education, attracted more participants. This took place at the same time as major trade union struggles were being waged – in the demand of steel workers for renationalisation of the steel industry, in the demand of the seamen for opening the books, epitomised in a strike pamphlet, *Not Wanted on Voyage,* written by John Prescott and Tony Topham, and in the demand of the dockers for workers' control in *The Dockers' Next Step – an Anti-Devlin Report,* challenging the Government's proposals for rationalisation.

In this situation it was not surprising, perhaps, that the next Workers' Control conference, in 1967 in Coventry, had 500 delegates and included seminars on the Health Service, the steel industry, the Coal Board, the motor industry, the docks, the aircraft industry, municipal buses, the big corporations, and education. John Hughes of Ruskin College introduced a session at the conference on the results of the Labour Party's study group on industrial democracy. He spoke on behalf of Jack Jones, who had chaired the study group and was to become General Secretary of the Transport and General Workers' Union and a strong supporter of the Institute for Workers' Control. Big questions were raised about the possible loss of independence by unions participating in management, and particularly in their having to take responsibility for decisions on redundancies. There was much discussion, therefore, at the conference about the presentations to be made by supporters of worker's control at the forthcoming Labour Party Conference in Scarborough. Ken Coates made a most moving reply to the debate, insisting on the importance of the demand for worker's control, that 'it is the practical foundation of the new life we are going to build together'. The conference ended with agreement to establish regional activities and conferences in Glasgow, Edinburgh, Cardiff, London, Nottingham, Manchester and Sheffield, and conferences and seminars on the following industries; aircraft, docks, steel, mines, buses, motors, and the student movement, with convenors assigned for each. First drafts of proposals for each of these industries were collected together with chapters on the controllers of the economy in private business and in government, and published as a paperback by Sphere Books in 1968 under the title of *Can the Workers Run Industry?* (available from www.spokesmanbooks.com).

A series of annual IWC conferences followed the founding of the Institute at the Nottingham Conference of 1968. The number of delegates exceeded one thousand, stimulated by a great number of pamphlets, particularly by Ken Coates, Tony Topham, John Hughes and myself. Not only the TUC, but also the Labour Party itself had entered the discussion of workers' control and its relation to the German system of *mitbestimmung* and British war-time Works' Councils. The IWC argument was concerned with preserving the independence of trade unions, and therefore critical of any scheme for workers' participation without built-in safeguards for the unions. This applied equally in the private sector and in the nationalised industries, where proposals were being advanced for trade union officials being considered for membership of boards of management at different levels. The IWC view was that workers' control should be seen as an extension of collective bargaining, not as an alternative to it. Critics of the IWC, in the Communist Party, for example, saw the whole IWC movement as a diversion from traditional trade union-organised resistance to arbitrary management.

What had begun to activate trade unionists in the late 1960s was the impact of capitalist reorganisation involving mergers and take-overs and accompanying closures. A paper which I had prepared on 'The Controllers of British Industry' was considered at the 1967 Workers' Control conference in relation to a paper by Tony Topham on the current role of the increasing numbers and importance of union shop stewards. Tony showed that trade union shop stewards' main activities were concerned not with questions of wages – less than a third of their time – but of job security, safety, and working conditions. At the same time, in 1967, Ken Coates was reminding us of Marx's warning to workers that fighting with the effects of their employment conditions was not the same as fighting the causes of those effects. 'A fair day's wage for a fair day's work' was a laudable aim, but it fell far below the revolutionary watchword, 'the abolition of the wages' system'. In responding to the 2011 riots in English cities it is worth remembering how it is that, even among those who are employed, most men and women at work are not in control of their activities, but involuntarily and arbitrarily subordinated to the will of an employer. Workers' control remains a claim to human freedom, and that was what Ken Coates was reasserting in 2003 in recalling the struggles of the 1960s and 1970s

In 2003, in *Workers' Control: Another World Is Possible*, one important contribution to the case for workers' control was added by Ken Coates in an essay on 'Education as a lifelong experience'. This essay not only expounded the case for life-long learning, through adult and continuing education, which had been the occupation of Ken himself and of many of those involved in the founding and development of the IWC; it also put forward a case for a different connection between work and education. In this vision the aim of education should not be a preparation for employment in a division of labour organised by owners and controllers of capital, but rather a development of the capacity of all men and women to build a co-operative commonwealth, in which human labour is not divided but united. The training of shop stewards in the development of workers' control could be seen in this light as something very different from the perfection of work study and scientific management espoused by F.W.Taylor in the Ford factories in the United States. Ken had found much evidence of the dehumanising of work processes in a book by my father, written in the 1930s, *The Machine and the Worker,* based on what my father had learnt from his students who had come on from working lives to Ruskin College, where he was the Principal. I found that things had not changed much when, in the 1970s, I became the founding Principal of the Northern College, the 'Ruskin of the North'.

After 1968, the responses of workers' trade unions through work-ins and sit-ins as the alternative to plant closure were proposed and tried. The most famous took place in 1971 at Upper Clyde Shipbuilders (UCS), in the shipyards on the Upper Clyde River in Scotland, but it had been preceded, in 1969, by a proposed sit-in at the General Electric Company (GEC) Merseyside plants, which Tony Benn visited when he was Minister of Technology. From that time on, Tony became fully involved in the work of the IWC and a close association developed between him and Ken Coates. Tony Benn had met the GEC shop stewards and been most impressed by their arguments, although the takeover was ultimately annulled. Two years later, as Shadow Industry Minister following the 1970 General Election, when the UCS workers, facing a shut down, voted unanimously for a similar takeover to that proposed at GEC, Tony Benn visited Clydeside and gave every encouragement to the shipyard workers. The IWC prepared pamphlets in support of a work-in and defended the workers' case in various forums, including the Heath Government Inquiry, which was established. An important volume was contributed by Robin Murray, who included a comparison with workers' control in the Split shipyards of Yugoslavia. A major victory was achieved when, in the end, public funding was obtained for a surviving nationalised shipyard complex. At the Labour Party Conference in1971, the visiting UCS delegation received an ecstatic welcome.

Workers' control is not something which is exercised in the abstract. It has to be related to fulfilling actual needs. These needs had been distinguished by researchers quoted by Ken as comprising all elemental needs of food, clothing and toiletries, environmental needs, such as housing, leisure, transport, and needs related to the person, such as education, sports, health, and cultural provision. Determining the priority of such different needs encouraged the concept of a social audit, which I examined in an IWC pamphlet in 1971 *(UCS – The Social Audit).* This considered all the effects on employment opportunities, benefit costs, lost taxation and so on of plant closures. This principle was then applied to other plant closures – coal mines in Yorkshire, steel works in Sheffield, Imperial Typewriter factories in Leicester and Hull, and Chrysler motors in Coventry. But the most imaginative application of this concept came from the Lucas Aerospace workers, who, beginning in 1974, drew up a detailed blueprint of the alternative uses in socially useful provision to which their skills could be applied. The whole range of products, from a hob cart for paralysed patients with spina bifida to coaches which could travel on road or rail, gave rise to many technological advances.

By 1974, enthusiastic support for workers' control came from the accession to leading positions in their unions of the two trade unionists, Jack Jones of the Transport and General Workers and Hugh Scanlon of the Engineers, who were strong supporters of workers' control. This led Harold Wilson to promise, in the General Election of 1974, to socialise the nationalised industries and set up a Committee of Inquiry on Industrial Democracy. This was duly set up under the chairmanship of Lord Bullock, who had been the head of an Oxford College. The IWC submitted its own recommendations concerned with preserving the essential independence of the unions. Stuart Holland and I had already presented to the IWC conference in 1973 a 'Model for Developing Workers' Control', where management would consist of equal numbers of representatives of employers, or of government in the case of nationalised industries, and of trade unions, with a chairman acceptable to both sides, subject to veto. Bullock's solution was to propose boards for companies consisting of equal numbers of representatives of shareholders and of trade unions, plus a third group of mutually agreed technical representatives. This proposal was countered by a highly divisive proposal that consumers should also be represented – but how could they be selected? Ken responded that the problem could be met by the establishment of planning agreements democratically reached by government consultation on specific issues. Little came of this on a national scale, but many local authorities, especially in the north of England, developed this kind of planning agreement. By 1977, some Yorkshire County Councillors associated with the Northern College were walking about with badges proclaiming 'The Socialist Republic of South Yorkshire'.

Efforts to proceed along these lines at a national level petered out under Callaghan's premiership in 1977-9, however, and the Bullock commission came to nothing. But a whole number of Workers' Producer Co-operatives were established, often with the direct ministerial support of Tony Benn, before he was removed from his post as Secretary for Industry. His successor, Eric Varley, had once written a pamphlet for the IWC on self-management in the coal industry, but did not follow that up with support for worker co-operatives. None the less, a good number survived for a period, such as the Triumph Meriden motor cycle company, joining other longer-standing co-operatives and worker-owned enterprises such as the Scott Bader Commonwealth, which operated a chemical factory in Wellingborough. Opposition to such developments came, perhaps surprisingly, from the Communist Party, which argued, going back to Marx, that such co-operatives formed a diversion from revolutionary aims. Other Marxists, such as the Belgian Ernest Mandel, a good friend of Ken's and mine, argued in favour of all attempts at social revolution, even modest ones, and this view was strongly supported by Ken himself.

When Ken comes to sum up the experience of those who struggled to realise the aims of the IWC, this is what he wrote:

'If they had any criticisms of democratic institutions, those criticisms would emphasise the need for fuller, not less stringent, accountability and openness. But they did show, both in their many brilliant individual initiatives and in their courageous joint activities, a burning need for quite new institutions, from which none could be excluded from the means to the fullest moral life available to any. The rebirth of socialism, which is what we are talking about, will be a true renaissance of individual human freedom, if it takes its growth points from such people as these. Precisely in so much as shipbuilders, coalminers, clerks and engineers are determined to widen the areas of choice and the material scope for self-fulfilment which are available in their own personal lives, and in so much as their combined actions serve these individual goals, the new commonwealth itself begins to come to life.'

This was written in 1981, in *Work-ins, Sit-ins and Industrial Democracy* (Spokesman Books), when there were three million unemployed under the new Thatcher regime, which had followed the disastrous 'Winter of Discontent' in the last year of the Callaghan Government of Labour, that followed Harold Wilson's retirement. What Mrs Thatcher set out to do was not only to destroy the power of the unions and the central role of mining and manufacturing in the economy, substituting services and, most particularly, financial services, but, above all, to replace the search by workers for individual freedom through a form of commonwealth with a purely individualistic freedom of private property starting with house ownership. 'There is no such thing as society, only individuals and families' she declared. And this became the accepted goal throughout the long Thatcher years, followed by Major's premiership, and no less enthusiastically embraced by Blair's New Labour. Recovering the goal of a commonwealth would not be easy, but Ken never lost hope.

The massive number of IWC publications during more than 20 years – the regular *Workers' Control Bulletins*, more than 90 pamphlets, dozens of books, the three annual issues of the 300 page *Trade Union Register*, with reports from several industries of strikes, sit-ins and other demonstrations of workers' solidarity, plus a diary of events and current employment and unemployment statistics – the annual conferences and innumerable seminars in different industries, all attest a vibrant organisation reflecting a deeply felt need that will not disappear.

Many popular organisations, concerned about climate change and community involvement, some under the leadership of 'Transition Towns', have recently been advancing a major challenge to the power of finance capital and, recently, Glasgow University students sitting in to protest arbitrary cuts made by management in their syllabuses, recalled the inspiration of the workers at Upper Clyde Shipbuilders, quoting from the University rectorial address, in 1971, of Jimmy Reid, one of the UCS leaders:

> 'Alienation,' he said, 'is the precise and correctly applied word for describing the major social problem in Britain today ... it is the cry of men who feel themselves the victims of blind economic forces beyond their control. It is the frustration of ordinary people excluded from the processes of decision making.'

Such memories do not die but are deeply treasured. The alternative to choice left to a market dominated by giant capital and its hangers-on is conscious choice by men and women in the situations that they know and come to understand case by case.

The Tyger

Tyger Tyger, burning bright,
In the forests of the night:
What immortal hand or eye.
Could frame thy fearful symmetry?

In what distant deeps or skies
Burnt the fire of thine eyes!
On what wings dare he aspire!
What the hand, dare seize the fire!

And what shoulder, & what art,
Could twist the sinews of thy heart?
And when thy heart began to beat,
What dread hand? & what dread feet?

What the hammer? what the chain,
In what furnace was thy brain?
What the anvil? what dread grasp.
Dare its deadly terrors clasp!

When the stars threw down their spears
And water'd heaven with their tears:
Did he smile his work to see?
Did he who made the Lamb make thee?

Tyger Tyger burning bright,
In the forests of the night:
What immortal hand or eye.
Dare frame thy fearful symmetry?

St Ann's

Bill Silburn

*Bill Silburn has taught at
the University of
Nottingham for many years.*
Poverty: The Forgotten
Englishmen, *a landmark
study co-authored with Ken
Coates, was published as a
Penguin Special in 1970,
and quickly became a set
text for sociology students
throughout the country.
Coates and Silburn's work
inspired 'St Ann's', a
documentary film for
Thames Television directed
with love and affection by
Stephen Frears. When the
film was shown at the City's
Broadway cinema in 2007,
with Coates, Frears and
Silburn all in attendance to
discuss, the venue was
completely sold out, and
further screenings had to be
scheduled. Many members
of the audience were
themselves from St Ann's, or
had grown up there. Later,
a similar event took place
at the Chase Centre in St
Ann's itself, attended by
some people who had
featured in Frears' film.*

I

The publication in late 1965 of Abel-Smith and Townsend's monograph *The Poor and the Poorest*, and the linked establishment of the Child Poverty Action Group as a campaigning pressure group, rekindled serious concern about the extent and nature of poverty in post-war Britain. As the conventional wisdom in the 1950s and 60s was that the combination of full employment and the institutions of the welfare state had effectively eradicated poverty, so the suggestion that relative poverty was widespread, and had become steadily more widespread throughout the 1950s, seemed to many to be shockingly implausible.

At the time Ken Coates ran an adult education evening class examining aspects of the changing social structure of Great Britain. For this group of students *The Poor and the Poorest* became both a highly topical and a potentially controversial text. After careful examination it seemed to the group that while the evidence (based as it was upon official government statistics) was compelling, it didn't easily square with the perception that most people seemed to be better off than they ever had been, the shops were full of both goods and customers, there were plentiful employment opportunities, in short that (in Harold Macmillan's quip), 'England had never had it so good'. One possibility, of course, was that poverty might be unequally distributed, concentrated in some less favoured regions of the country. If that were the case, then Nottingham, with its broadly based and buoyant local economy, was unlikely to be one such region, and consequently would not reflect the national picture. And so was set the scene for the recruitment of what eventually became known as the St. Ann's Study Group, determined to carry out an empirical enquiry to establish the truth of the situation as it was in one part of Nottingham. Little did anyone anticipate at this time that the work of the Group would continue for several years, and would lead to the publication of three local monographs (the first in 1967 and the third in 1980), and a Penguin Special that would go through three revised editions and is still in print as a Spokesman publication, more than forty years later; nor that it would be the subject of a radio-documentary by the Italia-Prize winning producer Charles Parker, and an hour-long television documentary, directed by Stephen Frears.

II

In September 1966 the study group started work, with Ken and myself as co-tutors. The student group was nineteen strong, full of enthusiasm for the project, and with a level of motivation that was to sustain them through long winter evenings trudging the streets and knocking on the doors of strangers. There were ten women and nine men, of all ages and backgrounds, and with very varied occupational and professional experience. Later on in this first phase of the research, when the time came to start to interpret our data, the diversity of the group was to be an enormous strength, adding depth and sensitivity to the analysis.

At the outset the plan was to carry out a city-wide sample survey, but we quickly saw that this was a task too great even for so highly motivated a team. However, several members of the group were familiar with the nearby district of St. Ann's, just a few minutes walk from our meeting-place, and they suggested we concentrate our efforts there. St Ann's was a densely congested and overcrowded slum area of dilapidated nineteenth century terraced housing. If there were to be pockets of poverty in Nottingham then surely they might be found in St. Ann's rather than in other more prosperous districts of the city.

For these practical reasons the Group decided to focus their enquiry on St Ann's, and spent the first few evenings familiarising themselves with the neighbourhood, and talking to as many local people as possible about their major concerns. Even at this early stage it quickly became clear that our initial preoccupation with measuring cash poverty was far too narrow a focus, and we needed to broaden the scope of the enquiry significantly. The topic that dominated casual conversations was the lamentable housing situation. The overwhelming majority of the houses in St Ann's were small terraced houses, the front door opening straight from the pavement into the front room; in most cases there was no bathroom or indoor sanitation, with just one cold water tap in the kitchen supplying all the households needs for water. Most houses were seriously damp, making it very hard to keep supplies of food or clothing in reasonable condition. Coal fires were the norm, although coal was both expensive to buy and dirty to store and use. Housing conditions of this kind affected the overwhelming majority of the local people (whatever their financial situation), and impacted upon their lives in so many different ways that the study group felt obliged to make it an important part of the enquiry.

And once we extended our interest to include housing poverty, so we became aware of serious issues of personal and public health hazards exacerbated by the housing and environmental shortcomings. These impacted most obviously upon the many vulnerable older residents of the district, but many younger women and children also suffered badly, if less visibly. In the same way and as the enquiry progressed, so the group became more conscious of the educational disadvantages suffered by young people living in seriously overcrowded circumstances, without any personal space for private study, either in the home or outside it. The women members of the group argued for attention to be paid to the plight of housewives and mothers trying to maintain family life in cold, damp and cramped conditions, and this often meant struggling to balance a tight family budget. Family budgets brought us back to issues of employment, and it became quickly apparent that while there were plentiful employment opportunities in Nottingham, including in the many small factories and workshops in St Ann's itself, rates of pay were often pitifully low, and many men relied upon long hours of overtime to earn a barely adequate family income.

In brief, the Study Group started to amass evidence of the multiple and often interlinked levels of deprivation that blighted the lives and hopes of those afflicted by them. The first report, *St. Ann's: Poverty, deprivation and morale in a Nottingham Community,* published locally in late 1967, tried to capture all these different but linked aspects as graphically as possible, but supported at all stages by strong empirical evidence.

III

The report attracted considerable local interest, with very mixed reactions, some strongly supportive and some severely critical. Some critics rejected our findings outright, and felt driven to question our motives for having undertaken the enquiry in the first place. More serious were those who criticised us for having identified St Ann's as the area we studied, as this might be seen as stigmatising to both the neighbourhood and its inhabitants; if that were so, then maybe our efforts would lower already low levels of local morale and pride. This possibility was a real one, but opinions were sharply divided about it, both within the group and beyond. But these different public reactions highlighted what many extended discussions within the group had already exposed, namely that our research could be understood from a number of alternative perspectives, and that each different perspective would alter how the data might be interpreted, the significance that would be attached to it, and the policy priorities and recommendations that might flow from it. One such difference of perspective was between those whose concern was with the specific local situation that had been studied and who were keen to explore the scope for local policies and activities that would ameliorate the situation, and those who understood the local data as being illustrative of a larger set of systemic shortcomings, requiring a broader and more fundamentally radical response.

Clearly the study was a local one, the conditions it described were experienced and felt locally, and the issues raised were seen as a challenge to local institutions and organisations. Most members of the study group (and most readers of the first report) had strong local connections and attachments, and were understandably keen to explore what local initiatives might address some at least of the issues raised by the report. Moreover an essentially local-centred approach was at the time reinforced by a number of developments taking place in the wider public environment. For example, the Plowden Report of 1967, `Children and their primary schools', recommended that extra funds should be channelled into primary schools in deprived local areas. This idea was eagerly taken up by some members of the group who were determined to ensure that the children of St Ann's would not be overlooked if funds of this kind became available. A little later, the Skeffington Report of 1969, `People and Planning', made a powerful case for much wider public participation in the development planning process, particularly at the early formative stage. This suggestion was seized upon by those who wanted to prioritise local and community involvement in all levels of public administration, and fundamental in the case of housing and town planning policy. Finally and more generally, there was throughout the 1960s considerable interest in the possibilities of local community development projects and programmes and, in 1969, Government funding was made available for a number of ambitious local schemes to explore the feasibility and potential of this approach. Even as we started our own research, a vigorous Tenants' and Residents' Association was established in St Ann's.

There was certainly much to discuss about local policies and strategies for improvement. Foremost amongst these was the City Council's decision in principle, made even as the Study Group was establishing itself, to comprehensively redevelop the entire neighbourhood of St. Ann's. This was a plan that would take several years to accomplish, and some people were worried that the sense of local community would be destroyed in the process. Meanwhile, a spirited debate took place between those in favour of radical redevelopment, and those who favoured a more modest programme of improvement of the existing housing stock. The needs of the youngest children and their harassed mothers encouraged an interest in establishing or extending pre-school playgroups staffed very often by volunteers.

But all the time there was a parallel set of concerns, based on the recognition that what was revealed in St Ann's was evidence of a much wider set of systemic and structural failures, of a kind that could almost certainly be replicated in other major towns and cities. The St Ann's study was an illustrative example of something that had to be seen as part of a much bigger picture, of a national and international scale. In this case, local initiatives might (quite properly) attempt to minimise the damaging impact of multiple deprivation on individuals and families, but would not directly confront the fundamental driving forces that generated the deprivation in the first place.

I think that it was this larger challenge that came to preoccupy Ken Coates more and more. While he was certainly active in local political life, rather too much so for the Labour Party hierarchy, he already had a long track record of active involvement in the wider Trades Union Movement, in the Peace movement and the Campaign for Nuclear Disarmament, in the Anti-Apartheid Movement, and an abiding commitment to expanding democratic practices in the workplace. The importance of the St. Ann's research was that it very vividly illustrated his understanding of the most insidious (though invisible) aspect of deprivation. This is the lack of opportunity the poorest have to make effective decisions about their own lives and well-being, the constraints on choice, even of the most mundane kind. For many of the mothers trying to stretch their budgets to the maximum, such meagre choices as they had usually served not to improve their situation, to enhance their families well-being, but to stop it from getting worse. Their lives were a constant struggle to maintain what little they had, with no realistic prospect of things getting better for them. And for many working men and women this democratic deficit was most marked in their own workplaces. Here they served their time, put in the hours, doing whatever they were told to do, little more than wage-slaves. This was not a matter that could be resolved locally, but one that required the widest possible mobilisation of ideas and individuals. In 1968, Ken and colleagues established the Institute for Workers' Control, and Ken developed his long and fruitful working partnership with Tony Topham. Towards the end of his life, as we see elsewhere in this volume, Ken wrote about the genesis of the IWC and the link he saw with the work of the St Ann's Study Group.

Twenty years later, as a Member of the European Parliament, Ken's tireless work on the global extension of human rights was, in a sense, the culmination of a mission that started during his years in the 1950s as a miner and union activist, that informed his long career as an academic and socialist thinker, and was exemplified by the collective enterprise of the St. Ann's Study Group.

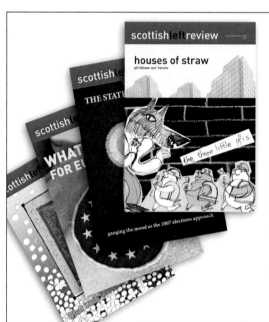

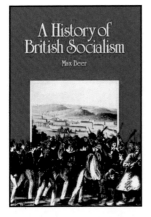

WHAT A STUNNING HONOR
IT IS FOR THIS OLD
CHRISTIAN IN HIS SUNSET
YEARS TO BE PUBLISHED
SO ATTRACTIVELY BY
WHAT IS POSSIBLY THE
MOST HUMANE INSTITUTION
ON THE FACE OF THE EARTH,
WHICH, PLANET IS NOW A GONER.
LOVE

DECEMBER 11, 2003

Ken Coates maintained a steady correspondence by fax with the author, Kurt Vonnegut.

About Ken

and some thoughts on the current situation

Regan Scott

For many years, Regan Scott worked creatively inside the Transport & General Workers' Union, latterly as its European Secretary. He collaborated closely with Ken Coates, particularly on the official history of the TGWU, together with Ken's co-author, Tony Topham. Regan actively participated in the work of the Institute for Workers' Control, as well as the campaign for European Nuclear Disarmament and other work of the Bertrand Russell Peace Foundation, to which he continues to contribute.

Pivotal people in popular and credible socialist politics, despite its sometimes bewildering and shifting '57 varieties', seem to possess one common and vital characteristic. They are the people to whom we turn to answer the time-honoured question: what is to be done? Ken Coates was evidently such a person, to friends, and, I suspect, also to enemies, who I have no doubt followed his public activities and writings very closely for their own nefarious purposes. Now we are without him we shall have to try to find some answers ourselves.

The need now for his natural leadership capacity is acute, for many routine reasons, not the least of which is the relative absence of left thinking and ideas and initiatives in this deep global financial crisis. This was just emerging when we collectively lost our Ken, so it is tempting, and perhaps a proper tribute, to try to imagine what he may now have been thinking and, particularly, with whom he might dialogue aside, of course, from his old economist colleagues Michael Barratt Brown and Stuart Holland, and his office team. That was certainly starting to be the case on the hugely complex issues of the global financial crisis, but there was, I believe, a set of prior issues about the structure of UK politics which had really engaged his attention as New Labour started to face a deserved failure and disgrace.

The set of issues can be expressed in simple questions: does the collapse of New Labour, and its assistance in eclipsing trade unionism, local democratic government and inner party democracy, mean that we have to start thinking about the prospect of an independent socialist party? And while this question is not an unusual one in the big historical sweep of working class and socialist experience, it soon transformed itself and became acute and urgent through its close link to the arrival of coalition politics in Westminster.

Political fragmentation had started to engage Ken's attention some time ago, not in any sense as a proponent of multi-party government, but more as a thinker about New Labourism and its fundamental transformation of Labour away from being a socialist party of wide class representativeness. The factual collapse of New Labour and the arrival of coalition politics underscored what may have been premonitions and ruminations. I feel we have a duty to explore them now that we face a newly configured national politics.

That Ken would have grasped this new reality quite quickly and naturally would have been no surprise. He had the rare capacity of raising central questions and often reformulating them at many key points in his life of activism. He did it about party, about war and peace, about union directions, about jobs and popular democracy and much else. That catalogue must include his early and pioneering work about core poverty in the heart of the welfare state in the sixties when almost everyone else thought the welfare state was doing fine by its clients.

Exploring the new reality would also have come naturally and even with a welcome because he had been watching the disintegration of social democracy and the cul-de-sacs of many left revisionisms for many years, looking for breaks and rejoicing when new forms of opposition arose to ruling classes across the world.

The Labour Party futures dimension would have been home ground for someone committed to political principle and truth rather than tribal loyalty, with long experience of Labour Party disciplinary pressures capped by his final expulsion as an MEP for, in effect, systematic opposition to Blair and Brown. It would have been intellectually comfortable territory, too, because of the pioneering work done in the early volume of the Transport and General Workers' Union history *(The Making of the Labour Movement)* with Tony Topham and myself. This found that the great dockers' revolt of 1889 had given the true stimulus to the formation by the new general unions of a proper Labour Party, and also to its quick linear succession, after Labour's turn to constitutionality, to the creation of the British Communist Party. All of that, to boot, through a common cohort of union and political leaders exemplified in the career of Tom Mann. A political story and dynamic not in any sense in keeping with the mainstream view of the Labour Party's origins as solid, natural and dominant and unchallenged within the working class. It was home ground, too, because of the experience of coalition and multi-party working in the European Parliament, where campaigns and projects cut through tribal party boundaries.

If the instinct for thinking about a new party formation after New Labour is accepted as a proper intuition about Ken's politics, the closely linked notion that coalition politics has arrived as the dominant structure of UK politics perhaps needs explaining and consolidating.

The arrival of core coalition politics?

Now looking shaky, having lost its 'newness', the coalition character of the UK government is still structural. Party loyalists are arguably now the only people who can sustain the view that a strong majority single party can take power again. Even if, against the odds, a majority party were to take office again in the next few years, the conjuncture – the awkward way history works – requires us to factor in the likely loss of Scotland to the Westminster Parliament. That would be a seismic event, whether it occurred directly by a straight independence vote, or indirectly through the political instability of Conservative Party absence in a freer Scotland. Add to that a not altogether unlikely Conservative coup to cut off Scotland and run a permanent Conservative England: that presents a truly determining set of circumstances. Whichever way Scots nationalism plays out, a much atrophied Labour Party north of the border, already the case because of New Labour's demise, would result in a profoundly weakened English Labour Party, given its traditional Labour MP dependency. So, overall, a picture not simply of the arrival of coalition politics in the UK, but also of party break-up because of Scots nationalism and resultant structural problems for the actually existing New Labour Party. Some conjuncture, indeed.

If this stark delineation disturbs, it may help to recall the character of Ken's recent politics, recent in the sense of the period from the formation of New Labour and his electoral emergence in the European Parliament.

Ken's European troubles bear recall: having taken a radical stand (as we did in the T&G) on the necessity of a socialist turn by the UK labour movement to European co-ordination, he was eventually expelled by Blair and his trains of camp followers for espousing quite sensible and moderate causes such as European full employment, human rights, collective worker rights, popular democracy through European free assemblies *(parlements)*, and crucially for my exposition, a re-uniting and restorative coalition politics across a broad consenting range of socialist groupings. A restorative politics for the old Left, for honourable social democrats, for Green democratic engagers, for independent Marxist parties and the much reconstituted Communist formations, especially in Southern Europe. To make the point abundantly clear: Ken had experienced and thought through in his own trajectory in the European Parliament a different perspective on future socialist politics while other folk of goodwill in the broad socialist community were continuing to hope that a simple two party/two classes-in-conflict model of modern politics would return.

Ken watched it all, keeping dialogue with many camps and trends and currents, but he was acutely aware that the collapse of the Soviet Union as a huge, hard political fact had really shifted the political goalposts. No longer did the Atlantic consensus have to make concessions to social democracy in case disaffected elements in the working class and its organic leadership started to consider more socialist alternatives. The crossing of this huge political threshold meant for Ken not recrimination, revisionism, regret and allegations and calumny, but the need for a new organisational principle for class-based socialist politics. Time and again he talked about 'combined and co-ordinated action' in the European space.

The big picture was not a simple opportunist product of New Labour's decline. It was rooted in close attention to political trends and movements across Europe. He was a good trend spotter and, while harsh about abstract political speculation and posturing, the babies stayed in his bathwater. He relished political analysis and political speculation, but it had to be concrete and graspable and intelligible.

This view was about how a rather beleaguered socialist tradition in Europe in general, and the UK in particular, formed up into a true 'big picture'. It took some time framing and shaping, and was based on almost compulsive corresponding and dialoguing with colleagues and experienced figures in UK and European politics. While the Right were into mould breaking – that is, breaking the Left's moulds, Ken was equally hard at work. And of especial interest, the notion of the break-up of the UK's dominant two party and majoritarian political structures was informed by the experience of former colleagues in the European Parliament, and through watching the work of the clever team running Scots nationalism and the rather more elderly socialists in Wales ploughing good furrows against Westminster and New Labourism in recent years.

There were echoes, to those who knew them, across most European countries of these breaks and experiments and trials. Ken knew them, followed them and found sustenance in them. They were the considerations that led him away from political retirement and isolation, or seeking Labour Party re-entry after he was expelled by New Labour. He joined a European coalition whose own politics were grounded in the twin facts of socialist commitment and the need for combination and co-ordination. This formation, the GUE-NGL (United European Left-Nordic Green Left) was not the only offer on the table. But it was the one which was historically proper and structured to fit his analysis and instincts.

Two missing cultures compound the challenges

Discussion and dialogue around this emerging picture often lit upon two other areas of change which needed to be faced and understood. It was recognised that they were important, even if it was not always clear exactly how they fitted into the big picture. That they were both secular trends in advanced capitalist democracies was obvious, as was the fact that both were more advanced – or regressed – in the UK than in many other countries.

One was the decline of an independent model of political democracy that had historically been embodied in the workings of the Labour Party within the confines of capitalist parliamentary democracy.

The second was the atrophy of public service and public sector culture, linked both to the virtual disappearance through privatisation of publicly owned industry and enterprise, and to the marketisation of direct public services at both national and local government levels.

Though only starting to be glimpsed as big issues, there are good grounds for thinking that Ken would have grappled with them and come up with some sort of project or initiative to explore them and seek progress. Discussion did cover ways for the NHS to be re-invigorated by a new, embracing self-management: an adaptation of the workers' control and industrial democracy agendas of the 1960s and 70s. And recent Spokesman publishing has covered sales of public assets and housing issues, in particular. I offer for discussion a few observations about them.

The Labour Party – a democratic party and constitutional force, or an electoral device?

What had become the problem with Labour's inner party structures? That they have changed profoundly cannot be questioned. And even more, perhaps, in inner party democratic matters than in the huge loss of core principles through the effective abolition of Clause 4. Ken and Michael Barratt Brown were amongst the first to see the full significance of the Blair/Brown attack on the Clause 4 public ownership principle. But what was not so clear at the time was that, once this basic policy and principle had been conceded to leadership prerogative, the whole of the traditional structure of policy-making by the membership who subscribed to party rules and principles simply went on the slide. Effective MP accountability to local parties soon disappeared; resolutions from local parties went nowhere; Labour MPs were barred from writing their own letters to constituents about policy issues; Cabinet government atrophied with a Prime Minister frequently not attending, preferring his office coterie. The ultimate logic, especially piquant for Ken and the Russell Foundation's peace work, was the apparently entirely personal decision of Blair to back Bush's war. The contrast in our lifetime is stark: Wilson faced Cabinet resistance sufficiently authoritative and a Party structure sufficiently powerful and independent that he dare not support the US in Vietnam with troops. To jump to life after Blair and Brown, the new New Labour leader has initiated a 'policy review' involving outside experts and establishment figures in an exercise which does not even seem to be nominally based in the Party's much reduced rank and file.

There were many huge changes. Electoral strategy took over policy formation and it was passed to focus groups and backroom experts; political heritage and obligation fell under the axe of the Milibands in their Downing Street think-tank, which required an innovatory future for all policy. The innovation principle meant that no past policy ever saw the light of day. Political tactics were replaced by a principle, if that is a proper term, of political triangulation, which meant that winning was what mattered, rather than sustaining and progressing a core issue. Brown got into bed with the bankers, distanced government monetary control from government itself, and prepared to survey and sell the nation's assets – the Domesday Project – with no mandate from either people or party, or indeed, as far as I know, from Parliament itself.

Electoral advantage, presidential political style, media power and a marketised, consumer culture moulding the parameters of political choice – whatever range of factors is explored to explain the change in the broader political process, it is hard to see how the Labour Party itself could now be in any sense an independent contributor to basic democratic life. That role had been, of course, in the view of many classical socialists and, more importantly, in active labour movement life, both a hallmark of socialist development, an ethical guarantee of basic socialist values in their own right, and a steadfast bulwark against ruling classes and their anti-democratic instincts. It was, inside the Party, the rock of democracy itself and the guarantor that Party leaders in power would represent, not just rule. That the Labour Party was a constitutionally plural party made up of balanced but asymmetric parts – core membership, collective union membership, and local government representation alongside parliamentary and socialist society elements – has virtually gone. It has become a parlous situation, obvious to socialists within and without the New Labour Party. Surely it follows that there is a new political fact in the labour movement, albeit an uncomfortable one for many people. It is that no Labour Party worth its name can be re-invigorated without a massive constitutional revival and re-inclusion of its several bases. One rose joined by however many other roses simply cannot add up to a flame, a sword and pen, for those who recall the iconography of our heritage.

The context and shape of contemporary political democracy is no aid either in the UK, though European parties seem to have held on to their constitutionalities much better. In the UK, Scotland and perhaps Wales apart, party democracy is weak across the national political structure. It has already been shown, very quickly, to be a far from robust animal in the Liberal Democrat Party, which had vaunted this dimension of its political culture. As the coalition programme crunches express and prominent commitments, for example, on student fees, parliamentary democracy looks to be vested more in the veto power of the electorate against majority party government than in the inner strengths of party democratic culture.

With such an overwhelming devaluation of democratic process in our public politics, perhaps a labour movement revival of inner party democracy could become an asset, rather than a liability in future, or is that too much to hope? For traditional socialists, inner party democracy was always a primary asset, however contested and pressurised it always was in the actual workings of the Labour Party. That said, the fact of the matter was that it *was* contestable under Citrine constitutionalism. That tradition was an operating pillar of trade unionism and local government, too, a connector, a transmission belt to working class political formation and the credibility of collective and unifying politics.

I think Ken had seen the seeds of political corporateness and authoritarianism growing in electoral politics a long time ago. His taste for free standing initiatives, for mobilisation and workshop debate, and open witness tribunals was frequently a counterpoint to the deficiencies and distortions of that strong old constitutionalism; for all that it would be an asset if it could be restored. How far back are we now when, in the New Labour party, throughout reconstituted local government and many other institutions, democracy and accountability are hardly spoken of. Even basic public information has to be wrenched from the hands of the powerful by a freedom of information law calibrating what ought to be matters of basic and unquestioned freedom. It seems that as ordinary people have lost their party and their voice, a new world of rights and law had to be invented as a countervailing force. That has to be welcomed, but as Ken knew only too well, it has not been a development that organises and mobilises: collective rights, and effective social rights, as modern unions know only too well, do not flow at all easily from legal processes and even basic human rights.

Although New Labour's former acolytes and proponents and backroom experts now freely talk of its 'demise' and 'decay', we should not be fooled. It was not just a 'third way' project which has run its course. What has been left is a substantial erosion of traditional labour movement assets, directly, deliberately and perfidiously caused by New Labour's hollowing out of a long British socialist heritage. This was an asset destruction of consequence internationally as well as domestically. It has been a development in UK politics much prized by longstanding American political strategy for transforming its major English-speaking ally's socialist party into a Democratic Party mould. If UK unions are now hard pushed to lay claim to the title of world home of trade unionism, the residual Labour Party must surely be in an even weaker position to claim credible title in the Socialist International, for all the doldrums of European social democratic and traditional left party politics.

Two structural changes: public sector and public service culture

Changes in global politics and the not unconnected changes in UK Labour Party structures and politics have evolved alongside other changes in the historic balance sheet of socialist experience. Of special note, I think Ken would count as crucial and complex and challenging the savage atrophy across society at large of the actual operating experience of public service and public ownership of industry and services.

The hollowing out and, in many cases, virtual elimination of public sector and service institutions in UK society and economy has been contested and challenged, and rightly so, not least by unions in the direct public services. These are vital struggles, but much of public culture, assets and worth has gone. It is this change which needs to be understood. The question can be put simply: what has been the effect of these huge structural reconfigurations on public consciousness of political and economic alternatives to the market society? As political generations age and new ones come along, traditional and largely popular experience of public ownership and public service can be seen as declining to a nostalgic minority experience. Their traditional roles erode as the stable, secure alternatives, withering away as the social anchors against a totally marketised way of life.

An example of the cumulative political effect is the banking crisis and economic slump. While the traditional Left's absence of effective policy alternatives has been widely noted, what may be equally if not more important is that the public at large does not seem to know that alternatives do exist and have actually existed. Angry and disabused they may be, but what natural presence has there been for different approaches to financial organisation and services? For public ownership and control interventions, for public investment and economic planning in place of huge subsidies for the very rich and powerful echelons of global capitalism whose greed has caused the crisis ?

The perception that there is an historic and structural problem here needs to be pursued, not least because so many actually committed and experienced socialists within the traditional labour movement seem to think it is entirely obvious and publicly visible that nationalisation itself might well be the solution. Well it might, and they would be right. But if large swathes of the working class and other ordinary segments of the electorate – the 'squeezed middle' for example – actually knew what it had meant and could mean today, the situation would not be, sadly, as it is.

The reduction of the scope of public service culture has been very profound, and more extensive in the UK than in many other countries. Public services are now composed largely of funded and budget-capped agencies run on market lines, working to consumer industry standards and modes. Look at the old core state-owned economic sectors and their traditional voice. They have gone, almost all privatised, except for nuclear generation and, for the time being, the postal services; and, as if to illustrate the point, the only exception a desperate but utterly pragmatic restoration of railtrack to public ownership at the taxpayers' expense.

I feel less able to set out the possible political culture aspects of globalised production and the concomitant loss of manufacturing industry in the UK and rich West at large, but instinctively feel that the loss of cultures of production to be replaced by cultures and labour markets of services and commodity exchange is of considerable importance. Perhaps this dramatic shift in our economic life should count as a third structural change. Its scope and scale have been extraordinary, challenging traditional concepts of economic management such as 'the commanding heights', influencing ownership and control in the national interest, stake-holding, social responsibility and social partnership – a catalogue extending from traditional socialist terms to the fashionable discourses of today. How real might they be in our changed economic conditions?

In the UK, and mirrored in much of Europe, de-industrialisation, which includes de-nationalisations such as the end of coal production, has left a tiny manufacturing base owned by foreign companies, except in military related areas which, in any case, are now internationally collaborative. Employment has shifted to market services. Unemployment and under-employment are deeply embedded. That's economic fact, and reasonably well understood.

What has not been understood, I fear, has been the effects on what used to be called 'consciousness', on cultural and community authority for production skills and the gravitational experiences of working people. What sort of social voice can the residual workforce exercise from the now narrow and often élite skill base and experience of marginalised production industry? What of the experience and voice of the much vaunted partners and stakeholders – workers, managers, investors, pension funds, and so on — in private companies in national political culture, when the big employers are retailer and service providers working frequently in very insecure and fragmented labour markets? And at ownership level, how can anyone identify with, engage with and formulate coherent protective and positive relations with companies whose managers are often simply of the high salariat and whose owners are fluid, international and impersonal? When one half of European corporate equity suffers ownership change in the equity and corporate bond exchanges every single day when the markets are open, who is the employer, who is the owner? It is not just labour law that needs to seek answers: labour movement organisation, politics and economic thinking need to face the structural challenges.

In our living communities, local government has been marketised, outsourced and agencied; its elected leaders become budget-constrained, executive commissioners, not accountable popular party leaders. Without primary accountable democracy and directly run services, how can ordinary communities make their voices heard and win resources for decent common lives? What of national economic strategy for jobs and sustainable growth when the British economy owns and places more capital abroad than it does in its home nation, and when the vast substance of national enterprise is foreign owned? And the bulk of corporate profit for multinationals is made from their foreign markets? What about Britain's unique NHS, due now to become a franchised brand 'delivered' by any willing provider under open market prices? Have we understood the change in culture and experience of an NHS which is no longer a common 'state' family of endeavour, and soon to become something like a Boots and Tesco NHS with hospitals branded by separate signs for 'customers' and private 'clients'; no longer the ordinary and universal patient in need?

What Ken had come to understand, I think, is that there was a whole range of fundamental political work to be done to re-establish socialist knowledge and credibility. That there has been a vast transformation of what might be called political culture, that needed to be assessed and agendas of change and alternatives formulated. How that might happen is not at all clear, but the principles of popular control and producer/worker control that mushroomed into labour movement life in the sixties and seventies deserve revisiting. Political conflict then was crowded, busy, chronic and crisis prone, and sometimes fast moving. I think Ken felt that it could be like that again. For all of the sheer scale of the challenges, and the need to understand them rather than deny them, he had a strong sense that political movement was subject to countervailing forces.

A political methodology within the heritage?

Part of 'what-is-to-be-done' for Ken was always, of course, straightforward: it was following, supporting and participating in the natural, basic processes of protest and opposition generated within the broad labour movement. The other part was more difficult, and core to the Russell Foundation tradition, which has typically participated in the mainstream of struggle and also tried to be a political pioneer and creative mould-breaker.

If there were an already-existing responsible and open labour movement debate – and debating structure – about what now needs to be done, I think Ken would have been busy at work exploring an array of approaches and ideas and initiatives. I have sketched some substantive issues and understandings which would have been, I believe, central to an emerging analysis. But to do his heritage justice, I think his distinct methodology and approach to politics deserves to be laid out to supplement what is obvious from the issues already discussed.

Little more than notes, this last section of an appreciation of his work requires a stylistic defence. Ken was frequently irritated by political analysis set out in bullet-points and numbered items, by formal ideas and programmatic thinking, preferring a silken and well-informed prose of discursive argument. But, despite his own high standards of writing, exposition and argument, he would sometimes recognise the merits of mechanical and pedestrian contributions by the less mercurial members of his team and many associates. I risk standing accused of that literary crime in the following rather plain notes. He was a hard task-master in the matters of argument and writing, and insisted that publication and the distribution of ideas, often through small vehicles, was an essential force in socialist political life. In the context of the debate about the future of New Labour, it needs to be recalled that he took on editing and publishing *New Socialist* for the Labour Party when its leaders no longer wanted the magazine: he started *European Labour Forum* magazine when much of the old Left was unreconstructed about Europe and labour leaders were following Atlantic and City of London mandates on the European Union.

But perhaps the most precious and distinct aspect of his approach to politics, a kind of methodology – not a term he would like at all, incidentally – was a grasp of the changing forms taken by important and principled issues as they evolved under political pressure. This cognitive capacity led to many innovations which developed existing issues rather than revising or rejecting them or avoiding them.

The Russell Foundation's signature working methods can be seen as consisting in a primary political *Gestalt* which always linked a big political picture with questions of connection to social bases of action and mobilisation. The mechanisms of activism were logically linked: networks of endeavour and open political debate and quality discourse. These were worked out alongside, but independently of, party organisation, but were also always closely related to party trends and political configurations. Institutionally, there was always a sense of the primacy of work organisation and the potential of strong and developed union politics, rather than the more mainstream view of the limited political culture of unionism. The relative independence of trade union political thinking was a precious asset of labourism. Geographically, there was a sense that European level organisation is an irreducible requirement of engaging with geopolitics and American dominion, particularly in British politics, even when the locus of direct conflict might be in Asia, or the Middle East, or South Central Asia.

Some of these approaches can be formulated more closely, and as such, may serve as guides for future work.

A principle of political development

The Bertrand Russell Peace Foundation, boosted by Ken's outlook and insights, was from the very start committed to radical understanding, including where necessary, and not always in line with the mainstreams of opinion, the consequences and characteristics of political change. It lit upon blocked developments in politics, falsely limited horizons, restoring principles that had been lost or set aside, speaking truth to experience. The Institute for Workers' Control was a political correlate to rising, mass unionism needing a voice outside formal Labour politics and a transformative vision beyond wages at the workplace. This work supplemented the analytical writing on trade unionism and its politics, but went further, adding an essential dimension to the struggle, configuring it differently to the impressive but limited mainstream. The END movement (European Nuclear Disarmament) strategically enhanced a locked-in British/American politics by opening up European territory just at the time when Cruise and Pershing missiles required placement on continental shores to reach their targets. Not against CND, but opening up a development of equivalent substance to the formation of the Committee of 100, which Russell helped establish in 1960. With the Socialist Group in the European Parliament, a European Left, and its European Left Party, started to occupy issues and develop agendas blocked by New Labour's stranglehold over Labour Party democracy in Britain and suppressed by European social democracy. This development, in turn, reconnected a strand of UK labour politics to the radical side of the European labour movement, taking us out of the earlier divisive and inward-looking impasse of Euro-communism. Earlier, and famously, the Russell Tribunal on War Crimes in Vietnam outflanked policy debate in the Labour Party, opposing the zero sum game of withering amendments of amendments and perfidious Parliamentary Party stratagems with a ferocious exposure through public examination of American dominion.

These examples show that political analysis and problem-posing could produce relevant and effective projects. In this persistent mode, Ken was not always correct about outturns, not always easy to argue with, but the method was a dynamic that led him, time and again, to develop initiatives and see them into organisational and, most importantly, mobilisation form. After that, history was the decider, of course, and while 'success' is not an easy term to apply to the great history of defensive and resistant struggles of socialist forces, these initiatives normally made a difference. They moved the cog wheels of history one or two notches forward, in stark contrast to so many formal socialist revisionisms and new approaches.

The big picture: American geopolitics

One of Ken's assets was a capacity to see the likely shape of big picture politics early on, and clearly, as political periods and epochs – the collapse of the Soviet Union – unrolled across the world. In his period, and ours, popular socialism saw some lifts and occasional brighter prospects, but many important assets were set aside and destroyed in the neo-Conservative era, and put far from easy recovery through what, in my trade union world, was called 'moving the goalposts'. The creative source of capitalist politics was always properly identified as the United States, whose own Left and dissenters were closely followed by Ken for their insights. But the axial role of the UK within the American empire was never far from his mind. It was not a global pessimism: so, the European socialist heritage was an irreducible part of the global algorithm, a kind of constant if very conditional potential for better things, and an essential referent for any UK political progress. As formal Europe seems immersed and threatened by crisis, no return to a socialism of Little England would have been in any way credible to him, though he had no illusions either that Brussels was where socialist politics might break out.

The irreducible base

While fascinated with high politics and trends, the formulation of his active politics did not involve élite interventions and the pursuit of high, élite influence, unless it could be used for express good purpose. The high moment of political processes was the movement of the base, not the posturings of the summit. Both levels have their own explanatory history, of course, but Ken's peculiar insight – or was it just hard experience? – was that the issue was not the problems of the base, or even the unattractive prospect of high struggle against often massive odds. The parameters of both could be quite wide and uncertain. The political issue was always what the connectors were, how a spark might travel outwards and upwards, how a conveyor belt – be it union organisation at branch and district level, or networking — how they might start bigger scale movements with a capacity for challenging where power really lay. Nothing unusual in formal political process theory here, but, sadly, a rare beast within labour movements. It is surely a partial explanation of why Ken was held in such high esteem by many traditional left leaders, especially in the unions, and not least in my union, the T&GWU. He had the knack, as an independent socialist with unquestioned and substantial inside experience, of somehow daring to shoot at the moon: it was a privileged position, I believe, which he earned and engineered. I recall fondly a comment from a meeting some years ago with the then T&G Deputy General Secretary, Jack Adams, in the Derby T&G offices: 'He's amazing – he never gives up, does he'. Need one add the gloss that this was not referring to political convictions! It related to the persistent aspiration to connect and engage.

Open dialogue and workshop organising

That dynamic could have played out in sectarian politics. Such a cul-de-sac was entered by many fine and committed people. Its seductions are strong, especially for people like Ken with more than adequate formal constitutional experience of socialist politics (early TU, CP, 4th International, and so on). That energetic apprenticeship happily produced an opposite effect: he came to set great store by spontaneous and open workshop politics, as opposed to the membership meetings run with Citrine constitutionalism and a world of final politics amended by yet another string of amendments. Democratic centralism must have felt very much the same as Citrine standing orders. But whatever their necessities and force, they often seemed to him, I think, to create more in the way of political manoeuvre than real political movement. For Ken the political problem was political movement, not political amendment. Like some of my better bosses at the T&G, he mused about how it might be possible to get all the rabbits in the field to run in a common direction, or perhaps, in the greyhound racing season, how to get the dogs to scent the rabbit. The big, positive vision was always of some kind of mobilisation, rather than the attainment of a paper-based, or administrative or even legislative compromise compressed into a professional, technical formula and likely disappointment. And in truth, apart from his own meticulous writing and editorial capacities, he was typically content for the 'workshop' or other clever people to dot the 'I's' and cross the 'T's', once there had been some dynamic established and sense of purposive assembly.

An independent – and interdependent – socialism

The politics of his final expulsion from the Labour Party highlight a basic, lifelong characteristic, at least once the early and natural Communist Party period was exhausted. Key aspects of his ceaseless projects and initiatives were determined by the inadequacies of the Labour Party and the conventional structuring of the labour movement, that rare and largely unified political animal which somehow achieved, perhaps with ruling class help, a single central organisation for its unions and local government power, and an electoral position never seriously challenged on the Left. Ken's politics lay *with* the labour movement, not with factions. With socialist independence, outside but not negative, supplementing and unlocking trapped forces.

It resonated with a particular sort of political syndicalism in some parts of the UK unions, and a strong independent campaigning tradition in what is now called civil society. Such was CND, such were earlier unemployed workers' movements and, more recently, the hugely successful Stop the War movement. Ken was deep into what might be called 'movementism' as a short-hand. His initiatives for a European Recovery Programme and full employment conventions, and the pensioners' and disabled people's parliaments in the European Parliament, were based on an open, rallying, representational and ancient model of *'parlements'*. The IWC was an open workshop movement. The early T&G history was tracing mobilisation and mass organisational formation.

These base level models of politics and its processes were not reducible to single issues, nor limited campaigns as such; nor were they, in my view, simply a matter of hard political experience about the inadequacies of the formal labour movement and the need to work independently.

So I would see Ken musing less about whether the post-defeat Labour Party could directly recover itself or be actively transformed, processes that do not seem at all credible or likely. His concern, I think, would have been more about how the cumulative independences from New Labour seen massively in the anti-Iraq War protests and in the disaffiliation of some key unions from Labour might develop and coalesce. And, cumulatively, about whether there might be a window for an independent socialist party formation in Britain – and, possibly residually, in England if Scots nationalism succeeded and coalition politics became the UK/Britain default. On the other hand, where a New Labour successor might grow – as an inside affiliate of a feebly recovering Labour Party or from outside — would be a central question. It would not be idle speculation: many, many tens of thousands of activists and committed people are denied a meaningful party.

What is different now is that independence and exclusion – by choice or force – from a Labour Party with only a feint heritage of inner party democracy surely mandates as terms of re-entry the re-institution of democracy as well as the restoration and development of socialist policy. That is a change of some weight compared to the days of 'policy capture' by conference and the rank and file asserting its primary authority over the Party and MPs and, indeed, Cabinets. Sadly, there is little sign of any understanding of this dimension of the heritage of a socialist labour movement as a precondition for mass party revival, so there is, to cite a Coates' favourite, 'much work to be done'.

Lifelong Comrade

John Daniels

John Daniels established the Russell Press.

It is a cause of much personal regret that I was not able to participate (to the extent I would have liked) in the many political campaigns and initiatives associated with Ken Coates. Apart from the usual commitments of family life, most of my waking and working hours were spent helping with others to develop one of Ken's many instinctive ambitions – the Russell Press. Over the years from its presses has flowed, hopefully, a profusion of eclectic radical texts that have made a difference.

I must have known Ken Coates from the age of about 11, which would place our meeting firmly in that tumultuous year for the Communist movement, 1956. This was the year of Khrushchev's Secret Speech, the Hungarian uprising, and also the year of Suez, and of what the history books tell us was a surprisingly spirited opposition by the Labour Party to one of the last overt splutterings of formal Empire. Nevertheless, it was the turmoil in the Communist world that pervaded the Daniels' household, so much so that the next-door neighbour was to inquire of the young schoolboy, 'What do you think of your Russian friends now?' Ken was one of the many frequent visitors who came to our home to discuss the turmoil within the Party. In particular, I remember one weekly sequence of visits which coincided with a series on BBC radio dramatising the debates in the infant Soviet republic. It must have been based on the Isaac Deutscher Trotsky trilogy, which was beginning to appear around this time. Unfortunately, I can find no record of such a series in the BBC Third Programme archive, but I well remember being intrigued by all these 'grown-ups' huddled round the radio in our smoke-filled dining room, to be followed by hours of animated conversation which kept the puzzled child from his slumbers. Of course, Ken's voice was often heard in the spirited debates that followed the broadcasts.

Ken continued to be a regular visitor, partly because of our privileged ownership of that not yet universal possession, the television set. Ken was a life-long film devotee and his attendance at the first TV airing of *Citizen Kane* initiated an interesting discussion on the morals of capitalists, 'yellow journalism', and US excuses for armed conflict – Tonkin Gulf and Iraqi WMD were yet to come. Ken did, during this period, make his own brief appearance on the small screen in a rather unexpected role, namely as disrupter of the equanimity of Hugh Gaitskell. The latter was engaged in a series of public meetings around the country 'saving the party he loved' from the arms of those misguided unilateralist disarmers, and one such gathering was nearby in Derby. Sitting watching ITV News one evening, my mother and I were treated to the sight of a bald head and a voluminous overcoat being carried out of the meeting by stewards and a young man remonstrating as he was physically pushed out of the venue. The interlocutor at the door was Ken who, along with my father, had attempted to make a verbal intervention in Gaitskell's oration, in defence of Labour Party policy, and for their pains they were both summarily ejected from the meeting.

Ken had left the pit after securing a scholarship to Nottingham University where he displayed such intellectual prowess that, on finishing his degree, he secured a lectureship at the University's Extra-mural Department. During his student days he became the secretary of the National Association of Labour Students and editor of their magazine, *Clarion*, but with the conclusion of his studies he was to immerse himself in the struggles of the local Nottingham Labour Party, becoming (much to the annoyance of the local civic leaders) President of the City Party. Much of the story of his expulsion from the Party and the devious role of the 'city fathers' is narrated by Ken himself in *The Crisis of British Socialism (1972)*, a book of essays on the first years of the Wilson Government. The Labour aldermen and some of the councillors were keen to rid the Party of those who would disturb their cosy do-nothing politics and moribund municipal flummery. Their inertia on comprehensive education and housing, often even at odds with official national policy, was exposed in a carefully tolerant, democratic manner by the actions of Ken as President of the City Party. This inevitably brought him into conflict with the Labour Group, described by Bertrand Russell at the time as reeking of the 'petty ambitions of tired and conservative local hacks'. Ken had also earned the disapproval of the national party hierarchy by his trenchant criticism of the Labour Government's direction in both national and international affairs, and particularly their abject public support of America's bloody intervention in Indo-China. It was, in fact, Ken's outspoken condemnation of the Labour Party's policy on Vietnam that brought him into contact with Bertrand Russell and his long association with the Bertrand Russell Peace Foundation. These two factions, the local councillors and the national party apparatchiks, had sufficient control of the party apparatus to suppress the legitimate right to dissent which should have been Ken's, and sustain his expulsion for some four years.

It was during this period that a discovery was made which was to transform the social life of the radical Left in Nottingham, for better – and for worse. Ken was now living in a first floor flat on Park Road, Lenton, courtesy of his live-in landlord Peter Price. Peter was a stalwart of CND and, at one point, a Nottingham Labour councillor and a companion with Ken in the struggles within the Labour Party. The house on Park Road was therefore a veritable magnet for all kinds of people whether local, national or international visitors. A visit to Park Road, to Ken or Peter, was a sure guide to what was preoccupying the Left. Naturally enough many of these lively discussions would be continued at a nearby local hostelry. One Sunday evening, the weather not inclement, it was decided that we would stroll to the nearest pub. Until then the 'nearest pub' had, in fact, been obscured from public view, being ensconced within a nest of terraced houses. All the housing had now been demolished, leaving one building standing on the rubble-strewn hillside – a humble watering hole by the name of the now politically incorrect *Black's Head*, subsequently to be known by all and sundry as the 'Ghost Pub'. That evening we discovered that the licensing hours, which were fairly onerous in the 1960s, did not seem to operate in this demolition wasteland. For about two years or more the 'Ghost Pub' (as its libertarian policies with regard to licensing hours became common knowledge) became a sort of social club for the Nottingham Labour Left. It must have been the only time that Ken spent so much time in a pub, as he was no drinker, but visiting celebrities were often treated to an outing with varying degrees of inebriation. Ernest Mandel was a strict orange juice imbiber, but Hugh MacDiarmid attempted to drink the pub dry – he failed. The many visitors to the pub provided Ken with much anecdotal scope for his impish wit. He was always a humorous man, ready to make fun of the human predicament with all its weaknesses, but he loved people and always engaged openly with them.

During this period he was working hard on a number of projects, amongst them editing and writing for the *The Week* and the *International Socialist Journal,* whilst also contributing to many other publications. Then there was all his university and WEA lecturing, plus instigating and directing with Bill Silburn that milestone amongst the studies of poverty in Britain – the *St. Ann's Report.* Perhaps Ken's most onerous labour was his participation in the exhausting and often pointless meandering arguments, common in 'groupuscule' politics, through his membership of that loose band of disparate Marxists cohering around the International Marxist Group (IMG), referred to laughingly by some as the 'Not Trots'.

Having helped to found the Vietnam Solidarity Campaign and by now a Director of the BRPF, Ken became involved in the debate within the IMG concerning the general political direction to be adopted. The primary national concern for Ken was the struggle for workers' control and its adoption by the labour movement as a policy for advance, as a way of switching the emphasis from the usual defensive posture of the labour movement (necessary as many defensive struggles often were). This brought him into a conflict of emphasis with those who saw the future only in terms of student revolt and the campaign around Vietnam. Inevitably, the differences led to substantive organisational questions within the IMG and there was a parting of the ways, with Ken forsaking forever that kind of politics.

Ken had always entertained the hope that *The Week* would one day dispense with the ink-smeared stencil duplicator for the equally inky but more visually appealing printing process. *The Week* metamorphosed into *The International* magazine, now the official organ of the IMG, which bore little or no resemblance to the spirit or content of *The Week*, whilst he moved with others to launch the Institute for Workers' Control. With the latter's pamphlets and *Bulletin,* together with the desire of the Foundation to launch a more regular and ambitious journal than their *London Bulletin* (which was to become *The Spokesman),* there seemed to be sufficient basis for the establishment of a printing press. As a result the Foundation took the decision to provide the small amount of capital necessary for its establishment.

The first premises were in cramped offices in central Nottingham, not far from Ken's place of employment at Nottingham University's Extra-Mural Department. The Press had to survive commercially, and its struggle to keep its head above water was a burden for us all. In the early days, Ken was a constant visitor, taking a very active role in advising and directing our efforts. The Press, however, did provide immediately a support and responsiveness to the campaigning activities of Ken and, later, the publishing endeavours of Spokesman Books. The Press was able to react to events swiftly, to underpin such initiatives as workers' factory occupations, the formation of producer co-ops, and the vicissitudes of the peace movement with timely pamphlets. Ken also had a genuine interest in the printing process, which manifested itself in his attention to cover design and his midnight searches through his bookshelves for illustrations and his editing of page layouts for maximum effect. This was on top of his normal workload of writing, researching and editing. Of course, as a keen bibliophile, he was aware of the life and work of that quintessential socialist, designer, artist and printer, William Morris, and was often to mention that dictum of Morris' 'no man is good enough to be another man's master'.

Others will have contributed memoirs of different times and areas of engagement, and I have necessarily restricted my contribution to Ken's presence in, and influence on, my formative years. His kindness and support, at times of personal travail, will be with me always, and I was by no means the only recipient of his innate good-heartedness. His prodigious political energy, together with an active interest in all manner of cultural, historical and scientific concerns, was only curtailed, sadly, in his later years by ill health. His enormous collection of books stands witness to the breadth of his knowledge and interests. He was always interesting, provoking and informative in conversation, but no armchair revolutionary. His legacy of campaigning commitment, erudition and insightfulness should galvanise us all into continuing the struggle to 'act locally and think globally', as he did. He always tried to examine new ideas sympathetically, but was scathing about mystifiers and betrayers who blunted the efforts of the Left. He never abandoned the central thrust of his ultimate commitment to arouse the idea of change within the bosom of ordinary working people. This was the aim: the means would vary tactically depending on both the times and the venue he found himself in. Many will recognise the merits of Ken's work over the years from his written, spoken and organisational endeavours, but only those who had the privilege to work with him over the years witnessed his tireless commitment, energy and humanity.

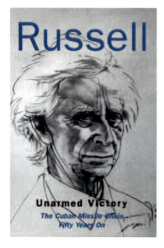

Russell

Unarmed Victory
The Cuban Missile Crisis
Fifty Years On

Unarmed Victory
by Bertrand Russell

Fifty Years On

The Cuban missile crisis of October 1962, more than any previous crisis, made the ordinary citizen suddenly aware of the ever-present danger of nuclear annihilation, and no sooner had the fright passed than it was renewed on the borders of India and China. Bertrand Russell shared these feelings, both the fright and the anger, but decided he must go on to turn concern into action. This book tells what he did in those frightening weeks, why he did it, and of the curious reception his activities had.

He asked Khrushchev not to challenge the US blockade of Cuba and Khrushchev acted as Russell had suggested that he should. This was exactly the action that the West had hoped for, but most people in the West still blamed Russell as too pro-communist because it was not by force that the result had been achieved. The same occurred in the Sino-Indian crisis. So the book contains a message of hope. Two precedents have been set for dignified and voluntary compromise in order to avoid nuclear war, and moreover the suggestions of a respected individual outside the battle were heeded. If we want a parallel we must look back to the thirteenth century, when Frederic II was quarrelling with the Pope and was ex-communicated. While ex-communicated he went on a crusade, but instead of fighting the Saracens, he negotiated with them. He secured far more than more warlike crusaders had ever been able to obtain, but he remained in bad odour with the Pope because it was wicked to negotiate with the Saracens. The analogy is very close.

ISBN: 978 085124 802 8 | Price: £8.95 | 156 pages

Spokesman Books, Russell House, Nottingham, NG6 0BT, England
Tel: 0115 9708318 - Fax: 0115 9420433 - elfeuro@compuserve.com

History will be kind

Tony Benn interviewed by Tony Simpson

The Spokesman met Tony Benn at his home in London in October 2011. We had arranged to discuss his long relationship with Ken Coates, and their joint engagement with the Institute for Workers' Control. Tony Benn kindly agreed that excerpts of the interview might also be used as an introduction to a new paperback edition of his book, Speeches, *which was edited by Joan Bodington and originally published by Spokesman in 1974, when the IWC was riding high. It's notable that the first selection in* Speeches *is entitled 'Industrial Democracy and Workers' Control'.*

Simpson: Ken Coates was very conscious of the Workers' Control tradition.

Benn: That was where I first got to know him well, when he invited me to a Workers' Control conference, in Nottingham I think.

Simpson: There's a quote in Ken's book *Work-ins, Sit-ins and Industrial Democracy*, which was published in 1981. He was comparing the difference between GEC (General Electric Company) in Liverpool in 1969, and UCS (Upper Clyde Shipyards) two years later. He said that there was a technical difference in the nature of the product, one was producing ships and the other was producing electronic equipment, but he also said that there was an important political difference. The Labour government had fallen and one of its most prominent Labour spokesmen had become convinced that the Labour Party's future depended on its willingness to become the champion of the cause of industrial democracy – he was talking about you. UCS was quite a triumph.

Benn: It was really. They succeeded in keeping the thing going. There was a lot of official support; Harold Wilson supported UCS, and the TUC was quite interested in it.

Simpson: The Scottish TUC ran a conference – it was a kind of inquiry or hearing. You refer to this in some of the speeches in your book.

Benn: Yes and the thing about Ken was that he really was a teacher of all the material you publish now and that he used to publish. He threw light on progressive issues that people may not have understood.

Simpson: I met him as a pupil in one of his WEA (Workers' Educational Association) classes; it was called '*Political Power in Britain*' and this was the autumn of 1979. Of course, it was a very interesting time to be sitting down with him and there he was convincing all these sceptics that what was happening within the Labour Party was for the good, that we were seeking to democratise this Party. In this respect the Institute for Workers' Control was again on a rising tide.

Benn: When I went to the IWC conferences, I noticed that many of the people there were Socialist Workers Party people. I was under extremely heavy criticism for not having done more when I was a minister, and I was slightly worried that I was a symbol of hostility that would embarrass Ken. But he rode over these things perfectly easily.

Simpson: The IWC was a place where the SWP, the International Marxist Group (IMG) and everybody else could actually come and have their say. We would give lifts to the local affiliates or activists in those organisations to various conferences

Benn: In a way, the Stop the War Coalition and the Coalition of Resistance were triggered and to some extent organised by the SWP people, or the ex-SWP people. The conclusion that I came to was that it is possible to be a socialist in the Labour Party, but the Labour Party is not a socialist party!

Simpson: Yes, and I think that's probably why Ken wasn't too distressed when he was expelled, because he was a socialist and his approach was a socialist approach. That's why he was an exciting person to work with because he did open up the possibilities of doing things in a different way. He had a different way of thinking, which is not so widely found these days, and what we're trying to do is to preserve and encourage it.

Benn: I think that if you argue for something but don't add the element of abuse it is possible, even within the Labour Party, to make a bit of progress. It's when political arguments become personal that you set up a lot of resistance. If you can get things going and interest more and more people, it builds up from underneath; all progress is made at the bottom, it's never at the top.

Simpson: Were there other openings for industrial democracy?

Benn: There was the one when I was at the Department of Industry – a little co-operative I set up called 'Meriden' [in 1975 at Triumph Meriden motorcycles near Coventry]. But you can't lecture people about the need for democracy; either they see the relevance of it and you encourage them, or nothing happens.

Simpson: And that's really what you were saying in a lot of these speeches, that you can't actually foist this upon people, it has to come from them – it's a demand or an aspiration.

Benn: And of course the attitude of the political leadership of the Labour Party to the Trade Union movement is stage one in a way, because if the trade unions feel that they have support from the Parliamentary wing, then that will encourage them to become more imaginative. Otherwise, they just fight on their own in a way that leads to division and no progress.

Simpson: Yes, I was struck by the contrast when you read Ed Miliband's speeches at the TUC or the Labour Party Conference. Ideas are not developed in these speeches; you have a series of headings with allusions to such things as co-operation or a new bargain. But there seems to be a real dearth of content.

Benn: If you're a political leader of the Labour Party, and you don't feel that the Trade Unions are your major allies, and that you must back them up when they take the initiative, you are really cutting yourself off, looking for support from the centre. And the centre never does really come your way.

* * *

Benn: When Blair became leader of the Party, he said 'New Labour is a new political party', which is a very bold thing to say – I never joined it, but it was really the beginning of a move by which Blair used the Labour Party for his own advantage … The Labour Party Conference nowadays is nothing but a press conference for the ministers who attend and a big trade fair.

Simpson: That's one of the most serious charges that could be made against the Labour Party.

Benn: That it has thrown away its democratic tradition.

Simpson: Yes, and it has extinguished much discussion, debate, as well as human fellowship, which is what brings people together.

Benn: There were fierce arguments about resolutions, but you knew that if you carried it, it became Party policy, and that protected you if they then abdicated it later, and put the leadership under some pressure.

Simpson: In 1982, you drafted a Bill prohibiting foreign nuclear, chemical and biological military bases in the UK, and it was to do with the conduct of foreign forces and the American influence. It was a part of the European Nuclear Disarmament Campaign. Later in the year, I remember seeing Robin Cook, who was active in END at that time, at the Party Conference in Blackpool. He was a bit perturbed that we had reference to this Bill in the resolution, which was carried by the conference. He said, 'the first one they'll arrest will be black American serviceman!' The Labour Party was actually onside for European Nuclear Disarmament, at the time, and Audrey Wise from the National Executive Committee came to the conferences.

Benn: Actually, the case for nuclear disarmament is so much stronger now than it was then – all of the old moral and political arguments have been supplemented by economic and practical arguments.

Simpson: Yes. If Ed Miliband thought about it, he could get ahead of that argument in the same way he got ahead of the Murdoch argument.

Benn: But in his decision to appoint his own Shadow Cabinet, rather than have it elected by Labour MPs, I can understand why he wanted to be free from the Blairite rump, but at the same time, to reject the accountability of the Shadow Cabinet to MPs is a bit strange really.

Simpson: Yes, and it's surprising how readily they gave it up. It tells you something about the Parliamentary Labour Party.

Benn: I think that the moves that are going on in the world, the world-wide occupation of capital cities that's going on now, is part of a stirring which is bound to penetrate the Parliamentary Labour Party from underneath at some stage. The 'anti-cuts campaign', for example, has been quite effective.

Simpson: It's surprising that the resistance isn't stronger at this point – the onslaughts are so comprehensive. Who would have thought they would not only fragment the health service but also do the same to schools and universities as well?

Benn: Thatcher said that she was the greatest defender of the NHS and that she would never let anyone do anything to it. This is very different from the Cameron line.

* * *

Benn: What do you make of this global movement for the occupation of capital cities?

Simpson: I think it's very interesting that it has kicked off in the United States – 'We're not going to move' – and it seems to me that the United States might be in the early stages of another revolution. I don't know the United States very well – I've been only once – but I've paid a lot of attention to how the US impinges on our life in Britain. I would be interested to know what your views are on what might happen there.

Benn: To mention the word 'socialism' in America is a risky thing to do. When I go there, I could talk about it easily, but I'm not vulnerable to the Tea Party in my local constituency or district. But there is quite an open mind among the intellectuals that you meet and among some American Trade Unions. That could mean something. And the tyranny of the International Monetary Fund, the Central Bank and the European Commission – none of whom are elected – has got us into a position where even quite progressive political parties are moving closer to what is a right-wing solution to all of these problems. So you do wonder whether this movement has some potential for shifting opinion.

Simpson: I was very struck by the state of decay of public amenities in the US – schools, colleges and the rest. It was the Boston Social Forum in 2004, which was just before the Democratic Convention. I stayed with a family (which included a teacher), and she was saying that the library budget had been cut several times, and the buildings were in need of repair. I think Coca Cola had a target to get 30% of the liquid intake of 16-18 year olds, and you could see it in the vestibule of the college. There were these ranks of Coca Cola machines, and also water machines, because they (Coca Cola) were selling water as well. Then there's the extreme poverty with people living under the flyovers, which must be much worse now.

Benn: That situation with the flood in Mississippi – you saw all of these poor, black Americans and it could've taken place anywhere in Africa, and you realise what a large percentage of people in America are on food stamps, or some form of low-level public assistance.

Simpson: My other impression of the US is that, in places, it is socially quite innovative, in that there is a sense of collective self-organisation, 'do-it-ourselves' activism, which is the same energy that drives the impulse to workers' control, that drove Upper Clyde Shipbuilders.

Benn: The end of the Cold War has made that easier because, if you talked about these things during the Cold War, then they said you were a Communist, and I think it's harder to write people off now for left-wing ideas in America.

Simpson: It seems to me that Barack Obama and his team are very much out of touch.

Benn: Yes, I agree with that, and I'm a bit disappointed. I never knew how much would come of it, but I thought that it was a very attractive campaign, and he beat George W Bush; then he made an approach to Russia, and made speeches about Palestine, and I thought something might happen. But now I think that he's a bit of a broken tool.

Simpson: On the question of occupation of capital cities, it's not actually confined only to capitals. There are people camping out elsewhere in San Francisco and Chicago as well, I believe. I went to Japan in August 2011 for the World Conference Against Atomic and Hydrogen Bombs, which they have every year in Hiroshima and Nagasaki.

Benn: Yes, on 6th August – I went to one of those once.

Simpson: It's a really powerful experience. You forget what it might mean, but after Fukushima, and the very high levels of nuclear contamination that are now being recorded in that part of Japan, it was a very telling time to be there.

Benn: There was a referendum against nuclear power in Italy.

Simpson: In Italy, there was a referendum that was against, and I think Germany has decided at Parliamentary level to phase out. France hasn't turned yet, as far as I know.

Benn: The French are very, very strong in nuclear power.

Simpson: I think there is a growing movement against, but it's the French who will build new reactors in this country if they get the chance. The extraordinary thing is that the Coalition Government has said not to worry about Fukushima, but to go ahead with the reactors as long as it doesn't cost too much – I think that is the position.

Benn: My view on nuclear power when I was put in charge of it as

Minister of Technology was that it was cheap and safe and peaceful. And I learnt by experience that it isn't cheap; in effect, it doesn't include provision for the storage of nuclear waste; and it isn't safe – look at Chernobyl; and it wasn't peaceful because, actually, the whole basis for nuclear power in Britain was to provide and have a nuclear relationship with America, under which they let us have the weapons and we let them have the plutonium from our nuclear power stations. And so I was converted completely in the other direction.

Simpson: The United States does have a disproportionate influence on affairs in this country.

Benn: Oh yes, very much so. The 'Special Relationship', and so on.

Simpson: It seems to me to be an abusive relationship, in fact.

Benn: The day I was elected to Parliament for the first time (which is a day I will never forget, the 30th November 1950), Harry Truman made a speech saying that he might use atomic weapons in the Korean War, and Attlee actually flew straight to Washington and stopped it. Later, Eisenhower didn't support us and forced Eden out. And then, at the time of the Vietnam War, Wilson absolutely refused to supply even a band of Scottish bagpipers to go to Vietnam, and that's the real basis of the 'Special Relationship', candour between friends. But we are very dependent on the Americans, for their nuclear weapons, and I think that is a factor that influences all Labour leaders in anything that might lead them into conflict with the Americans.

Simpson: That's a case of the 'Emperor's New Clothes', because they could well do without the next instalment on Trident. It serves no military purpose, as Mountbatten said. It was actually Ralph Miliband, Ed's father, who discussed with Ken Coates the European Nuclear Disarmament approach. In the late 1970s, Edward Thompson approached you to lead a campaign against cruise missiles and their installation in this country. Edward and Ken talked to Ralph and, between them, came up with this idea of a broader European Nuclear Disarmament approach. Politically, it was very significant; and I think, in some ways, it helped to create the context for Gorbachev's emergence in the Soviet Union, and the subsequent Intermediate-Range Nuclear Forces Treaty, which removed cruise missiles and SS-20s, among others.

Benn: I think that any international campaign for a progressive purpose, whoever you're working with, adds enormously if you've got more countries involved.

Simpson: The reason I mention the Japanese is because the contacts I made there, who had been visiting the United States, have been joining the occupations in San Francisco and Chicago, which are sympathy actions with the occupation of Wall Street. This idea is bouncing around the world in different places; there's an occupation in Nottingham outside the Council House in Old Market Square – it's fairly modest, but it's an expression of solidarity. I think what it does is expose the fact that people have realised that there is the 1 per cent who are extremely rich and look after themselves, and then there's everybody else. These are very powerful statistics. We used to say, '7:84' [7 per cent of the population have 84 per cent of the wealth]; now it's '1:99'.

Benn: That is a class element coming into discussions now, which I haven't seen at the level it's going on now for a long time.

Simpson: The class is much broader, and I don't think there's been any cogent political response to it, that I have seen as yet.

Benn: If you talk in class terms, it's an acute embarrassment to the Labour leadership, and to Miliband; therefore, they can never quite identify themselves with movements of the kind that are progressive in character.

Simpson: Ken Coates was rather well-disposed towards Ed Miliband.

Benn: I voted for Ed. I thought he would be a better bet than David. He worked in my office, doing work experience years ago.

Simpson: He came to Nottingham with his father, Ralph, in the 1983 election. Ken was standing in Nottingham South and Ralph was on the doorstep for half an hour talking to one family, and Ed was running from door to door. We reminded Ed of that when he came to Nottingham during the leadership election. I feel that he has heard a lot of the arguments about workers' control, about what went wrong, about democracy. But his formation has been governed more by his experiences in the 'Blair machine', and it seems to me that, underneath it, there's the possibility of somebody with rather more decent instincts. I think that has shown itself over Rupert Murdoch; he did very well in handling that and he didn't just do it in interviews; he did it in the House as well, and wrong-footed Cameron at every turn.

Benn: Ralph, whom I knew very well, once said to me, 'My boys say to me, "Dad, if we did what you want us to do, would it work?" And I used to say, "Sometimes my children say that to me as well".' That suspicion of a radical idea of a certain element is a problem. You have to overcome it by showing that it does work and that you can make a lot of friends this way and make a bit of progress.

Simpson: Ken did try to make contact with Ed, because Ed also showed courage in standing for the Leadership against his brother. That took some pluck.

Benn: He won because he appeared to understand what was going on in the country.

Simpson: Yes, that's right. He wasn't supposed to win, of course; and that did create a little bit of space for a short time. What will happen now – who knows? But I do wish that he would address the nuclear weapons question.

Benn: So do I.

Simpson: Because Trident is seen publicly as so pointless.

Benn: Well, we can't use it, we don't need it, we can't afford it and we don't actually have it because it's American.

Simpson: Yes, and they may build it to a specification that they won't be able to use in the boats the British Government are building. It's completely at the discretion of America.

Benn: The Americans want us, not because they need us in economic and military terms, but because if an American president can say he's working with the British, then that makes the prospects of succeeding rather greater. After Vietnam, they were very frightened of being alone.

Simpson: I was reading an article by Amanda Bowman from Atlantic Bridge, Liam Fox's organisation. It seems it was principally a US-based thing and Liam Fox was the UK end of it. She wrote this article in the *Washington Times* at the time of the general election of 2010, saying how Cameron's election would be important for the United States for a number of reasons. She said that more than a million Americans work in the United Kingdom – I'm not sure whether that figure's right – it sounds very high to me. Clearly, this organisation had the role of smoothing Cameron's path in the United States.

Benn: I think one of the reasons why Cameron wouldn't want to cross Barack Obama would be in case it interfered with the supply of weapons, and of course, the Tea Party group in America are based on the Boston Tea Party as a sort of revival of the anti-colonial liberation movement. It's quite interesting.

*   *   *

Simpson: I get the increasing impression that we need a European Network for Peace and Human Rights again. Ken started this in 2002 when you came to Brussels and I'd like to try and revive that partly to resist the expansion of NATO – Sweden is expected to join. I have been trying to find people in Sweden who would campaign against it and they said they tried but they couldn't convince people to do so. I was told Norway was the 'good boy' of NATO by some Norwegians. I don't buy that. Actually the Norwegian air force was bombing Tripoli; they were also using their maritime aircraft.

Benn: In this recent event?

Simpson: Yes. They were using the maritime planes to monitor the long coastline. The British services train in the north of Norway. They have radar trained on the Russian missile testing sites. It is an important part of the so-called 'Missile Defence' infrastructure. I don't want Sweden to go in that direction and I don't think it would be good for Europe if Sweden does go further in that direction. The reason I don't think it is good for any of us is because it is about surrounding Russia. It is about intimidating Russia. They would say it is about containing Russia if they were candid, but they probably wouldn't be that candid.

Benn: The trouble is that Yeltsin and the Gorbachev crowd really began to introduce neo-liberalism into the old Soviet Union.

Simpson: Yes, indeed.

Benn: And although I am all in favour of good relations with the Russians because I think the Cold War was a total diversion from what had to be done, it might be difficult to find a progressive point of contact. It might be that it would be seen as just absorbing the old Soviet Union into the European Union.

Simpson: Russia is enormous. It is one seventh of the land area of the planet. I think it would be difficult to absorb into anything. It is just enormous, but it has common interests. Its people have the same needs and the same motivations. It is true that there has been the most extraordinary neo-liberal explosion and some of the people who have enriched themselves now live in London and probably launder their money through the City. My impression is that British policy towards Russia, Foreign Office policy, is two pronged. On the one hand it is publicly hostile, I think, but on the other hand it is more hospitable to Russian capital and to some of those who have fallen out with Putin.

Benn: It is encouraging the very same tendencies.

Simpson: I can understand the Russian alarm at being encircled in the way that they are. Now that Latvia, Lithuania, Estonia are all part of NATO, and they were pushing for Ukraine and Georgia to go in that direction as well, which was a much more pivotal development.

Benn: I always hoped that China might turn out to be a progressive influence but I am not sure how easy it would be to bring that about.

Simpson: Ken always had some hopes of China. It is certainly a powerful influence.

Benn: Oh yes, the shift to the East in global terms is on a huge scale.
Simpson: Ken took a keen interest in Bukharin.

Benn: I remember, yes.

Simpson: And eventually Bukharin was rehabilitated; I think it was 1989. His son, Yuri Larin, is a celebrated artist now in Russia. Ken met Su Shaozhi, the Director of the Institute of Marxism, Leninism, Mao Zedong Thought, and Su translated his book about Bukharin into Chinese. Of course, Bukharin was an advocate of the new economic policy and the operation of the market within certain limitations. China has gone way beyond that now. I know Ken was somewhat ambivalent about whether what he'd done was beneficial or not in the greater scheme of things.

Benn: Someone will pick it up and be influenced by it. I think to get the name of Ken and Ken's contribution known more widely would encourage a lot of people, and so this should be a popular book. He was a teacher really, wasn't he, at heart?

Simpson: Yes.

Benn: That was his start as a WEA teacher. Has anything ever been written about Ken?

Simpson: No that I am aware of. I don't think there has been any kind of comprehensive assessment of his life and I'm not sure we are in a position to do one yet because there are quite a lot of aspects of his life that we don't know about, particularly during the 1950s and early 1960s. The thing about Ken was he would always take on the big issues and he wasn't afraid of them. There was extraordinary courage.

Benn: And imagination.

Simpson: Yes. He would make things easier because he expressed them in human terms. 'Think globally, act locally' was really a very appropriate motto for him. He had an appreciation of formation, by which I mean political formation. He would look to see where people's roots were and where they had come from and this would help him, for example, to understand the French Socialists and their various groupings. He always spoke in the collective, it was always 'us' and 'we'. I remember the IWC was attacked on Question Time one night by a retired general – you were on the programme – and you said you would come back to this question about the IWC. It was attacked for being subversive and encouraging strikes and all kinds of things. You gave a very passionate defence of the work of the Institute for Workers' Control because it was in that spirit of personal liberation and it was to do with people's direct experience.

Benn: And encouragement.

Simpson: Yes. In the 1973 strike there was all this work the IWC did on the coal stocks. It used to be said that the IWC knew more about the coal stocks than Heath did. I don't know whether that was true or not but the outcome was successful. How do you remember Ken now?

Benn: I knew of him earlier, obviously, and during the coals stocks thing I think we made a lot of use of that during the campaign. I knew his name and a little bit of him and then when I went to Chesterfield he approached me and we had long talks and I was much encouraged by it and I co-operated in some of the projects he had in mind and I believed very strongly in him. I was very sorry he got expelled from the Labour Party, although I understand why, but I felt that he had been picked out.

Simpson: There was a democratic issue, which was to do with the closed list system for electing members of the European Parliament and that was all about controlling who got in. Although he wasn't going to be standing again himself he had a fair point to make on that question.

Benn: I remember him making a passionate speech at Chesterfield Labour Party on that question at the time, which I noted in my diary. He was a friend. I think of him as a friend, somebody I trusted and encouraged me. We could discuss things together and I think history will be very kind to Ken. I think he will be seen to have had a much more important role than people understand.

With grateful acknowledgements to Katie Jones, Abi Rhodes, Stephanie Sampson and Alva White for all their help with recording and transcribing.

MAY DAY GREETINGS
from
Unite – Britain's biggest union
defending jobs, protecting pay

Len McCluskey
General Secretary

Tony Woodhouse
Chair, Unite Executive Council

unite
the**UNION**
www.unitetheunion.org

Reviews

Was Tito One of the Greats?

Geoffrey Swain, *Tito: A Biography,* I.B.Tauris, 2011, 232 pages, hardback ISBN 9781845117276, £59.50

It so happens that I met Tito on one occasion, an official reception in Belgrade in 1946, to which I was invited as the Executive Assistant to Mihail Sergeichic, the Chief of the Yugoslav Mission of UNRRA (United Nations Relief and Rehabilitation Administration). I introduced myself and my wife to be, who was with me. She was a doctor who had worked in hospitals in Italy treating wounded Yugoslav Partisan soldiers before we could enter Yugoslavia. For this work she had been awarded the Tito medal, which she wore under the lapel of the jacket of her uniform. The pin of the medal showed through on the outside of the lapel, and Tito bent the lapel over to reveal it. He smiled, and said in Serbo-Croat, 'Very good; thank you dearly,' and passed on to the next guest. I tell this story, not as self-aggrandisement, but to make a point about Tito's character. He was not only a very brave and thoughtful man, but quite exceptionally concerned with human relationships, especially, I must add, female ones, and my-wife-to-be was strikingly good-looking.

This book is one of a series on post-1945 Communist leaders, written by academics; this one by the Glasgow University Professor of Russian and East European Studies. It is not in any way a rounded biography of the man, but an interesting study of Tito's disagreements with Stalin, his attempts to work with Khrushchev, and his commitment to a form of Socialism based on the needs and interests of ordinary working people like Tito himself, in his upbringing as a skilled mechanic.

From my point of view, the book misses very much of importance in Tito's life. There is scant reference to his successful war-time collaboration with the British Military Mission to Yugoslavia, there is not a word about the role of UNRRA in the relief and rehabilitation of Yugoslavia after war-time destruction, which Tito's relations with the British made possible, and almost no recognition of Tito's important role in the creation, after 1968, of the 'non-aligned powers' as a response to the Soviet and Western Blocs, and nothing about the launching of the world-wide 'Round Tables' held in Cavtat.

These omissions greatly weaken the book, and we should still rely on Phyllis Auty's biography and Steven Pavlovich's *Reassessment*, together with Stephen Clissold's documents and Milovan Djilas's writings, all of which Swain draws on very heavily. The success of Tito in rallying resistance to the Axis invasion of Yugoslavia was recognised, after two or three years, by the Allies who began to drop supplies to the Partisans and not to the Chetniks, representatives of the exiled government in London and their General Mihailovich. By 1944, at the time of the landings in France, Churchill informed the House of Commons that 'the Partisans' guerrilla army of over a quarter of a million men were holding in check fourteen of the twenty German divisions in the Balkan peninsula in addition to six Bulgarian divisions and other satellite forces – which could otherwise have been supporting the German resistance to the Allies in France. Geoffrey Swain makes no mention of this.

In internal affairs, Swain's discussion of Tito's quandaries about combining political control of social development with economic freedom, for workers in their unions to manage their own businesses, is interesting, and these problems have a relevance far beyond Yugoslavia in the 1960s and 70s. The key question relates to investment funds. Too much freedom for workers to draw on these gives to particular businesses and regions excessive resources at the expense of the country as a whole. Too little freedom discourages workers from increasing productivity and developing new opportunities. The Soviet system gave too little; the central bureaucracy decided everything. The Yugoslav experiments with workers' self management tended to give too much freedom, and when this had to be reduced, successful businesses and regions complained bitterly.

Tito had to exercise a continuous balancing act in his rule between the Soviet style bureaucrats led by the Serb, Alexander Rankovic, often referred to as 'right-wing', and the workers' control enthusiasts led by the Slovene, Edvard Kardelj, referred to as 'left-wing'. The balance was the more difficult to maintain because of the different interests of the several national states of the Yugoslav federation. Slovenia and Croatia in the north and west were relatively rich; Bosnia, Montenegro and Macedonia in the south relatively poor. Serbia stood in the middle in both wealth and geography. The southern states needed, and at first received, considerable subsidies from the centre. It is a great weakness in Swain's book that, in the lengthy discussion of Croatian separatism, this difference in wealth is not recognised, nor the fact that the gap between rich and poor widened over time, as world prices for the products from the north, mainly manufactures, improved, while world prices of raw materials, the chief products of the south, declined.

The separate nationalist tendencies in Croatia reached a crisis point in the 1970s when Tito had to use the full powers of the League of Communists to discipline Croatian officials and their supporters, particularly among the professors and students at the university of Zagreb. They had the support also of some Belgrade professors and the magazine *Filosofia*.

Tito had hoped at different stages to find support for Yugoslavia's form of socialism in the revolts in Hungary and in Czechoslovakia, but both were put down by Soviet military intervention. Tito's work for a world non-aligned bloc attracted support in Asia, Africa and Latin America. This was the so-called Bandung Pact, based on a first meeting in Bandung, Indonesia, in 1955, attended by Tito, Nasser, Nehru and representatives of 29 other countries. Bandung remained as a symbol of Tito's commitment to a form of social development that was neither American capitalist nor Soviet communist. His travels around the world established him arguably as one of the great figures of the Twentieth Century, along with Roosevelt, Churchill, Lenin, Stalin, Mao and Mandela.

Toward the end of Tito's life in September 1976, a conference was organised by the Yugoslav League of Communists in the Croat resort of Cavtat, drawing on contributors from many countries to found a movement called 'Socialism in the World'. 'Round Table' meetings, as they were called, were held every year in Cavtat, and a journal carrying all the contributions was published. I was able to attend many of the annual meetings until they ended in 1988. In bringing together leading socialist writers from the whole world, including the Soviet Union and China and other Communist lands, Tito's legacy was kept alive.

The break-up of Yugoslavia during the 1990s cannot seriously be attributed to Tito's policies. The absence of political democracy to be combined with economic democracy made Yugoslavia particularly prone to separatism, but it was the intervention of outside powers – Germany in Croatia, the United States in Bosnia, and NATO in Serbia that destroyed Yugoslavia, as I have argued in my 2005 book, *From Tito to Milosevic* (Merlin Press).

For the rest of Tito's life – he lived until 1980 – he maintained his position of head of state and party, with the full use of his several residencies, but increasingly surrounded, according to Geoffrey Swain, by yes-men, and holding to a Leninist, if not Stalinist, view of the dominant role of the League of Communists. On the other hand, before he died, Tito established a rotating system among the several republics of Yugoslavia for the leading position of head of state and party. It was a major concession, and should have settled the matter in a democratic fashion, but for foreign intervention.

Mrs Harriman, wife of Averell Harriman, the US ambassador to the Soviet Union under President Roosevelt and at one time US representative in Yugoslavia, recalled in her memoirs that Tito confessed, in the late 1970s, that 'Apres moi le deluge!' I often wished that I had found out from her whether it was said with a straight face or with a twinkle in those pale blue eyes. In talking to Phyllis Auty, in October 1968, Tito said, 'I have tried to devote my life to the good of the people and the country'. It is quite unjustified, in my view, that Geoffrey Swain should end his biography on a sour note; that 'Tito failed to recognise that it was time to end the dictatorship'. It was, but he was too old to do it. It could have been left to his followers, but most of them, unfortunately, fell to the blandishments and armed intervention of foreign powers.

Michael Barratt Brown

Unslain

Yanis Varoufakis, *The Global Minotaur: America, the true origins of the financial crisis and the future of the world economy*, Zed, 2011, 264 pages, paperback ISBN 9781780320144, £12.99

As the world economy spirals into deeper crisis, one sometimes wonders how distant generations, perhaps in three or four millennia (and, of course, ecological or other apocalypse permitting) might perceive the ideas that precipitated this current situation. What strange cult required the worship of 'free markets' through the sacrifice of human needs? What set of exotic beliefs required huge tribute to the priesthood of the idolatry of money while those who cater for the health and wellbeing of the overwhelming population of society became increasingly submerged in deepening impoverishment? These fancies run through my head as the latest report of bankers' bonuses is discussed on the radio playing in the background. The thoughts are, however, framed by reading this book by Yanis Varoufakis, a Greek economist attempting to understand the current economic crisis through an exploration of the longer term development of global capitalist economy.

While Varoufakis' analysis ranges across the history of capitalism, and its periodic crises, an important question around which the book is framed concerns the capacity of the US economy to remain hegemonic after the collapse of Bretton Woods and the post-war economic consensus in the early 1970s; the 'balanced disequilibrium' of continuing US hegemony following withdrawal from the gold standard of the dollar in 1971. For the first time, such global power was held, not by the producer of the world's surplus, but by the consumer of the world's surpluses. This appropriated surplus has then been used to fund the US – and by proxy the UK – in spiralling deficits. It is here that the book gets its title, metaphorically linking the rush of world tribute to Wall Street with the human sacrifices to the half-bull, half-man of Cretan mythology. The story of recent global economy, therefore, becomes:

'... a tale of unbalanced might stabilized and sustained by one-sided tribute; of a hegemonic power projecting its authority across the seas, and acting as custodian of far-reaching peace and international trade in return for regular tribute that keep the beast within.' (p. 25)

The book is framed around the emergence and decline of the 'global minotaur', and presents a clear and very readable account of the background to the '2008 moment' of the banking crash. It is, in fact, the rewriting of a more technical thesis in political economy – *Modern Political Economy*[1] – by Varoufakis and colleagues successfully transformed into a very readable account for a wider and more general audience than academic economists.

With backward glimpses of the enclosure of land and other factors in the emergence of capitalism, and the drive for commodification, the inherent problem with capitalism, against other modes of production, is that it requires payment of wages before realisation of the product, indicating the growing importance of the finance sector. The significance of Wall Street, and its satellite in the City of London, is shown to grow in importance in the Twentieth Century following the power of the new mass production industries. Post-war US global policy became buttressed by their support for the economic development of Germany at the centre of the European Union in the West, and of Japan, as default for China, lost to revolution early in the process, in the East. The flaw in the post-war settlement – for Varoufakis as it was for John Maynard Keynes – was the absence of a global recycling mechanism which would allow trade imbalances to be held in check, a problem which was to reappear for the EU and the euro four decades after it had caused the collapse of Bretton Woods and the dollar gold standard. Capable of capturing the inflows of financial tribute, the audacious outcome of US policy makers led to the financialization explosion with, effectively, the privatization of money in the creation of newer and more exotic products inflating the bubble. Any growth in US economy following 1971 came from the extension and expansion of credit rather than any real economic improvement; and as many recent commentators have indicated, the imagination of financial institutions was increasingly focused on masking the fact that risky credit was increasingly extended through such loans instruments as collateralised debt obligations.

There are limits to the metaphor. Varoufakis is an excellent guide through the labyrinth of modern political economy, clearly linking the post-2008 period to the longer dynamic and periodic crises of capitalism without the cataclysmic or dogmatic tenor of many such works. But there was no Theseus to slay the minotaur; the 2008 banking crisis may have wounded the beast, but did not kill it. The Global Minotaur may have been 'critically wounded' (p 21) but perhaps the inference from Varoufakis, that this is likely terminal, was an understandable misdiagnosis. The beast has proved much more dogged than anyone might have thought only a year or two ago. In fact, rather than anyone rendering the death blow, the main efforts have been to attempt to heal the beast so that it may emerge stronger than before.

Varoufakis is weakest in attempting to articulate the possible alternatives. What is certainly noticeable is that there has been no alternative articulated within the hegemonic powers. In the crisis following the crash of 1929, to which 2008 is often compared, we see the expression of Keynesian views as the very emergent orthodoxy which was to create the foundation for the Global Minotaur. Neo-liberalism, the post-1971 orthodoxy, remains intact and, unfortunately, echoing some distant sentiments, there appears no alternative. It is only the 'occupy' movement, which has sprung from the bowels of the global labyrinth, that has appeared to challenge this shoring up. From outside of the orthodoxy – of economics and the Left – and reflecting the scream of the global underbelly, it is from the tent cities that have sprung up that any sense of alternative has emerged.

Alan Tuckman
www.workerscontrol.net

Note

1 Varoufakis, Y., Halevi, J. & Theocarakis, N. 2010, *Modern political economics: making senses of the post-2008 world*, Routledge, London.

A New Revolution

Paul Mason, *Why It's Kicking Off Everywhere: The New Global Revolution*, Verso, 2012, 238 pages, paperback ISBN 9781844678518, £12.99

This is probably the most important book for *Spokesman* readers that I have read for a long time. Paul Mason is the economics editor of the BBC's Newsnight programme and author of *Meltdown: the End of the Age of Greed.* In this book he describes his experiences of actually participating in the protests, disturbances and occupations in London, Athens, Cairo, New York, Oklahoma, Kenya, Spain, Palestine, Libya and Manila during the revolutionary year of 2011. His aim was to discover the nature of the people revolting and their motivation. What is so important is that these popular movements were not part of trade union or other collective organisations, but of individual protests linked up by the new technological means of communication; Facebook, Blogs and Twitter.

What is astonishing about Mason's evidence is the sheer numbers involved – not thousands or even tens of thousands, but hundreds of thousands, even millions in London and Cairo. Nearly all the protesters everywhere, moreover, are young – between 15 and 30 years of age, linked together by their new mobile phone access, which enables them to know what others are doing all over the world, well ahead of the journalists' reports and the police mobilisation. On motivation, Mason shows that the destruction of life opportunities in the economic crisis, plus the obvious growing inequalities between the super-rich and the poor, lie at the heart of the protests. But it is the sudden change in life chances for so many that made 2011 a year of revolution at the time of a growing sense of individual consciousness. 'I am not myself. I am someone else who was born today' was what a young woman in Cairo's Tahrir Square told her mother.

There is no ideology driving this movement, but there are ideas of social justice and fairness circulating widely among the social media, and it is the expanded power of the individual that is being celebrated. What is new is that the urban poor, jobless youths, street traders and women are refusing to be labelled 'chavs' ('rednecks' in the US) and demanding their rights, and, as Mason adds, 'in every garret there is a laptop'. At least, the first phase of democratic revolution can be achieved, Mason insists, by getting inside the decision cycle of those in power. It changes the balance of power between the leaders and the led. It is not anarchy, as Durkheim saw it, but a mass refusal to co-operate.

For many young people the situation in 2011 was nothing less than disastrous. Unemployment in Greece had begun to rise; by 2011 youth unemployment was running at 46%. In Portugal and Ireland and soon in Spain, there was the same situation. So long as the Germans refused to underwrite an issue of Eurobonds, it was inevitable that Italy, France and others in the Eurozone would join them. The UK suffered a peculiar problem. Jobs created under Labour had been filled by European immigrants. Resentment was directed at the immigrants, but the lost jobs in the public sector under the Coalition's austerity measures were not being made up for in the private sector and unemployment, especially among young people, created much disillusionment. Among new university graduates there was special anxiety, because they had assumed that their future was secure. Those families with mortgages living on their credit cards found that their assets were worth much less. Some joined the protesters and even the looters.

The extent of Facebook and Twitter grew exponentially. By 2011 there were 750 million users of Facebook, launched in 2004, and Twitter, launched two years later, had 250 million users in 2011 sending out a billion tweets a week. 'For me it's second nature' said one tweeter, quoted by Mason. 'I tweet in my dreams.' The new technology provides a social network for quite individualistic purposes, which challenge the old methods of organisation – parties, trade unions, leaders, hierarchies – and leave wide open what type of economy would start the transition to sustainable and equitable growth. Mason wants to remind us that Marx's aim was not class solidarity but the liberation of human beings. He quotes Marx writing in 1841,

> 'Human emancipation will only be complete, when the real individual man has absorbed into himself the abstract citizen; when as an individual man, in his everyday life, in his work, and in his relationships, he has become a species being.'

Mason's studies in the United States reveal the disillusion with Obama and an even deeper sense 'that we were great once'. Obama's concessions to the Republicans over health and cuts in relief for the poor are bitterly resented. Mason quotes the remarkable two week occupation of Madison Capitol by students and young teachers threatened with reduced salaries and loss of their trade union negotiating rights. Others followed. Moreover, current high rates of unemployment are contrasted with the wealth of a few and the huge numbers of unregistered migrants – perhaps 20 million, mainly from Latin America. The idea of occupying space has taken on everywhere, from Tahrir Square to Syntagma Square in Athens, the US capitols, Wall Street and St.Paul's in London. It is a statement of power in a powerless situation for most ordinary people, and it has a certain resonance.

The penultimate chapter of the book looks back in history to consider earlier similar periods of protest. Mason singles out not only the Roosevelt years of response to the last major economic recession in the 1930s, but also examines the revolution of 1848, syndicalism in the 1900s, and the student revolt in 1968.The Communist Manifesto of Marx and Engels, published in 1848, opened with the words, 'A spectre is haunting Europe: the spectre of Communism'. It is not yet haunting Europe today, but the seeds are being sown at least in Europe, the United States, Latin America and in the Arab world.

Mason's last chapter looks at the developing world of Asia. There is surprisingly little about China and India, but a fascinating study of the Philippines, sub-titled 'Slum dwellers versus the super rich'. This reaches the strange conclusion that the skills of the workers in the slums are an essential element in a certain form of capitalism, which cannot at all easily be replaced. Only in the more advanced countries do the 99% of the population have the education, the ingenuity and the intelligence to challenge the life destroying impacts of poverty, inequality and the monopolised power of the 1% élite. Mason ends his book with the lines he heard being chanted in Cairo's Tahrir Square:

> 'When the people decide to live,
> Destiny will obey,
> Darkness will disappear
> And chains will be broken.'

Michael Barratt Brown

* * *

In *Spokesman 115*, Michael Barratt Brown reviewed Susan Williams's book *Who Killed Hammarskjold? The UN, the Cold War and White Supremacy in Africa* (Hurst & Co, 2011). He has subsequently drawn our attention to the *London Review of Books* of 26 January 2011 which carries two letters, one from Ms Williams and the other from Rolf Rembe in Stockholm, that, he says, tend to confirm 'the doubts of many in a position to know concerning the verdict of pilot error reached by the colonial authorities and suggest a deliberate operation to stop Hammarskjold's UN mission organised by those authorities'.

The Blood Never Dried

Richard Gott, *Britain's Empire: Resistance, Repression and Revolt*, Verso, 2011, 480 pages, hardback ISBN 9781844677382, £20.00

The author admits that this book has been many years in gestation and it is, perhaps, therefore serendipitous that its publication should roughly coincide with various 'worthies' pontificating on the supposed positive outcomes of empire. The latest contribution to this nostalgic genre is BBC television's *Empire,* written and presented by Jeremy Paxman, who darts about the globe meeting people who reveal, as he expects, that the Empire was not such a bad thing after all, marvelling at this plucky island race which managed to subdue a quarter of the world's population. Previously, Gordon Brown has suggested that 'British values', as represented by the British Empire, have 'influenced the rest of the world' and 'we should celebrate much of our past rather than apologise for it'. Niall Ferguson, in his book *Empire: How Britain Made the Modern World,* quotes approvingly the comment of one Seymour Martin Lipset to the effect that 'British colonies had a significantly better chance of achieving democratisation after independence than those ruled by other countries'. The assertion may be dubious to say the least, but if we broadened the scope to take in other forms of social turmoil that the British Empire has left in its wake then the picture gets decidedly bleaker. The problems of India's partition and Kashmir, Ireland, Cyprus, Palestine, South Africa and Ceylon (Sri Lanka) can, in part, be ascribed to the manipulation of existing social divisions. A conscious policy of 'divide and rule', with one group often selected, in preference to other ethnic or religious groups, for imperial policing and the lower echelons of the state bureaucracy, left behind fractured societies, riven to this day.

The book does occasionally touch on such questions, but it is above all a purely factual work cataloguing the response of the colonised to the colonisers, during the period 1755 to 1858. Its central theme shows that, far from welcoming their new masters, the indigenous populations were unambiguously and uniformly hostile – and with good reason. In North America the French and British colonisers, together with the slave-holding newly founded settler republic, the United States of America, vigorously pursued genocidal policies towards the Native Americans. As Gott explains, even the use of primitive germ warfare was employed with attempts to infect Native Americans with smallpox and other infectious maladies of the Europeans. This was apart from the usual forms of rapine inflicted on the East Coast tribes which succeeded in decimating their numbers in a relatively short time. One cruelty that the author highlights is the British army's recruitment of black slaves during its struggle with the infant North American settler republic. These former slaves were to be granted freedom on the conclusion of the war, but for obvious reasons, as the war was lost, they had to be found a home where they would not be subjected to punishment and renewed slavery. A large body of ex-slave soldiers ended up in Newfoundland, later to be shipped to West Africa to form the British Colony of Sierra Leone, as it was felt that these black ex-soldiers would be able to withstand the vicissitudes of the climate and the hostility of the existing residents. In fact the British were keen to try the experimental colonial manoeuvres in Sierra Leone because of the necessity of finding a home for domestic convicts and other malcontents after American independence had made their dispatch there impossible. Finding a new 'gulag' and hastening the cessation of using prison hulks, a perceived temporary measure, was certainly for government a powerful stimulus to voyages of 'discovery' such as that of Captain Cook's reconnoitring of the Pacific.

The book covers many of the machinations of the British conquest of Australasia and the tensions between settlers and the authorities. The author highlights the harsh treatment of the Aborigines and Maoris, which in the case of the indigenous inhabitants of Tasmania resulted in complete extinction. There is an interesting quote from Captain Cook on the life of the Aborigines which his fellow countrymen were about to destroy:

> 'They live in a tranquillity which is not disturb'd by the inequality of condition: the earth and the sea of their own accord furnishes them with all the things necessary for life; they covet not magnificent houses, household stuff etc.,'

The British Empire did them no favours – contrast the above with the blighted communities of the present day. Gott gives a detailed account of the development of colonisation and the various armed conflicts with the Aborigines, which were both brutal and very one sided. There is also a chapter on Maori resistance in New Zealand but, unlike many of the countries that made up the Empire, there was little or no serious competition from other European foreign powers for hegemonic control of Australasia. This is not the case with most of the other chapters, which are woven around the conflicts of the European powers who were frequently at war up until the Congress of Vienna in 1815. These wars in particular form the back-cloth to the many slave rebellions in the Caribbean and also the British conquest of India. In particular, the Napoleonic period and the rising of the Haitian Black Jacobins and the impact of the French Revolution are integral to the twists and turns of British expansion in the Caribbean. The appeal for slavery to end in the Americas was also capitalised on by the British in its shifting alliances with slave and Maroon rebellions.

The French in particular, but the Portuguese and Dutch as well, were in direct competition with the British for control of India. This was finally resolved in 1757 by the battle of Plassey, and from this point the book takes us through successive military campaigns to crush Indian resistance. The British relied on native recruits known as Sepoys for the majority of its troops and it was necessary to keep a firm grip on their discipline and loyalty to the Raj, infractions of which were punished with much brutality. Even before the

Great Mutiny of 1857, revolts in the ranks were by no means rarities amongst both Hindu and Moslem recruits. The most feared punishment practised by the British was 'cannonading' where the unfortunate victim was tied to the muzzle of a field gun and blasted to smithereens. This form of punishment was used extensively during the mutiny of 1857, which is charted in detail in the book including some photographs.

This is an extensive and comprehensive work covering resistance in many other locations including Ireland, West Africa, South Africa, Afghanistan, Burma and Sarawak. It does not touch upon the economics of the Empire in any detail or the ideological ramifications of denying freedom to so many people and nations, but it exhaustively shows the events of resistance over a particular period in history. It is to be hoped that the author intends to bring the book up to date with a successor work taking us up to the eclipse of formal empire at least. Because this volume ends in 1858, the great omission is, of course, the so-called 'scramble for Africa' in which Britain added even greater swathes of territory and encountered further indigenous resistance. The book is, however, a mine of information and a counterblast to those who would seek to gloss over the horrors of the British Empire.

Paxman in his televised oration contrasted two aphorisms, describing the Empire as an entity on which the sun never set or the blood never dried – this book confirms the latter.

John Daniels

America's Wars

Vijay Mehta, *The Economics of Killing: How the West Fuels War and Poverty in the Developing World*, Pluto Press, 2012, 250 pages, ISBN 9780745332246, £14.99

Vijay Mehta is the chair of Uniting for Peace and founding trustee of the Fortune Forum charity. This interesting book of his has a bad title. 'Killing' implies single murders, as in the Danish book and TV series, 'The Killing'. It is perhaps understandably used here, because Vijay Mehta wants to emphasise the preparedness of the US secret services to use killing to dispose of enemies, as in the case of Lumumba, Hammarskjöld, Guevara, Allende or Letelier. The sub-title of the book is better; the book is about 'fuelling war', mostly by the USA.

Propaganda presents the United States as the great champion of peace, democracy, free trade, food aid and open government, but the true situation revealed in this book is very different. The sums spent by the USA on preparing for wars and conducting them are astronomical, exceeding all the combined military expenditure of other nations and three times what would be needed to provide food and water for the poor people in the world, and end their poverty. And the figure of $550 billion spent by the US in 2008, as Mehta explains, did not include 'military assistance', balanced by the value of US equipment sold to clients such as Israel and Saudi Arabia, nor the sums provided in other US budgets such as the Forces' pensions and compensation for injury.

US Governments, Mehta argues, have used their military power to coerce other governments, and particularly those with oil reserves and other key raw materials, to make these available specifically for US use. This is most evident, as Mehta shows, in US support for dictatorial and corruptible regimes in the Arabian peninsular, in Latin America, and in West Africa. It has also been evident in the actual wars fought by the USA in Vietnam, Iraq, Afghanistan, Libya, parts of Latin America, and in the threat of war in Iran. What Mehta shows most convincingly is the disdain shown by US Governments to the peace-making role of the United Nations.

Authority of the Security Council is supposedly required for any national military action. But the US has embarked on the deployment of armed force without UN support in Yugoslavia, Iraq and Afghanistan. John Bolton, President Bush's Ambassador to the UN, described the top floors of the UN building in New York as 'dispensable', and even President Obama's former Defence Secretary, Robert Gates, is quoted as berating the European members of NATO for failing to spend more than 2 per cent of their national wealth on weapons and people to use them. The survival of a North Atlantic Treaty Organisation (NATO) after the demise of the Soviet Union's Warsaw Pact is shown by Mehta to be due to the US Government's need to maintain a large military force.

Mehta discusses at length the rationale for United States' militarisation. It is supposed that military technology is the key to all technological development. But this is only because the most powerful corporations in the US, such as General Electric, Boeing, Raytheon, and Halliburton are heavily involved in military production and supply. It is in this context that Mehta concerns himself so much with the growing threat of China to US dominance in every spectrum, land, sea, air and space. China is shown to be carrying out every type of espionage to obtain the secrets of US high technology; what Robert Gates is quoted as calling 'America's crown jewels'. The US buys consumer goods from China but pays with dollars, not with advanced US producer goods. How long the US debt to China can be allowed to grow is a big question, which Mehta does not seek to answer.

The concluding chapter of this book, an Epilogue on 'The Path Ahead', is the least satisfactory in my opinion. One observation which I would dispute is that a major task is to demolish economic theory. Not all economic theory is wrong or harmful. I would exempt Keynesian economics from Mehta's denunciation. The proposal to disband NATO I entirely agree with, but where should we start? The web used by the social movement, micro finance and Fair Trade are all movements recommended for support, and I would agree. The Appendix contains an extraordinarily valuable list of Global Peace Organisations, with their addresses. But the big question remains – how to develop a movement in the United States which would challenge the present power of the great corporations to determine US foreign policy and to influence US election results.

Michael Barratt Brown

Socialist Register

Leo Panitch, Greg Albo and Vivek Chibber (editors), *The Crisis and the Left: Socialist Register 2012*, Merlin Press, 320 pages, hardback ISBN 9780850366815, £50.00, paperback ISBN 9780850366822, £15.95

The latest edition of the *Socialist Register* continues the theme of the 2011 edition and is again devoted to the continuing global crisis of capitalism. Historically the *Register* has always had, and rightly so, an international sweep but has often found room for the inclusion of a number of articles on British themes. It is with some nostalgic recognition that, perhaps, over the years, these have diminished. Could this be realistically justified on the grounds of the particularly uninspiring terrain the British Left has been forced to inhabit for the last few years? All three of the present editors are based in North America, where the sub-prime match lit the global debt conflagration, and certainly it is there that the Occupy Wall Street movement has demonstrated the power of innovative protest. The editors confront what they stress in the preface is the continuing audacity of the neo-liberal schema: the pursuit of policies, in the face of crisis, which are so draconic that they may yet inspire generalised unrest. They could even turn around the largely pedestrian and down-right cowardly response of social-democracy in most of Europe – witness the heartening mass participation in the 30th November one-day strike in Britain.

Certainly the British situation deserves special analysis for the reason that, ever since 1979, it has been a test bed for the implementation of the neo-liberal agenda, under both the Conservative and New Labour governments. The Thatcherism of the 1970s and 80s sold off the utility companies and, with its cunningly divisive sale of council housing, induced a bubble in owner occupation, paving the way for rampant housing inflation and the consequent housing shortage. In fact the first article in the book is one by the Anglo-American political geographer and proselytizer for Marxian economics, David Harvey, who in an interesting and informative article traces aspects of the roots of the present crisis partly in the urban post-war expansion of the suburbs and urban development in general.

Harvey takes issue with some Marxist economists who, he considers, underplay the causal role of housing and the property market in capitalist crisis, preferring to concentrate on under-consumption and the falling organic rate of profit as the primary culprits. Land price bubbles have been a common feature of American economic history, and of many other nations. In the US, prior to the present crisis, we had the Savings and Loans débâcle under Reagan, the Japanese property bubble and, to round it off nicely, the sub-prime mortgage banking crash. In our own neck of the woods we have had the neo-liberal approach to housing foisted on us, with the 'freeing up' of rent control and the selling off of council housing, all of which helped to sustain a housing bubble until the banks realised that their number was up and had to go cap-in-hand to the governmental begging bowl. Harvey makes a very thoughtful case for adding urbanisation to our understanding of both boom and bust and shows how the continuing sub-prime crisis has led to a massive transfer of wealth from the poor to the rich.

This urban crisis suggests another area where the struggle for social redistribution of wealth and control over our own lives should take place, namely the built environment, through tenant groups and the like. We have seen this in action in the US with Occupy Wall Street groups going to the aid of sub-prime homeowners about to be evicted. Harvey also discusses the credit system and how it has the dual function of being a conduit for production, but is inevitably used for facilitating speculation and the accumulation of capital. In the US and elsewhere naked class warfare is being fought on one side by an alliance of finance capital, developers and construction companies against whose predatory practices the isolated home owner is no match. The article has a section on the Chinese housing and property boom, and here again Harvey notes the danger signals, comparing it with Florida of the 1920s, which JK Galbraith has noted in his book *The Great Crash 1929,* 'contained all of the elements of the classic bubble'.

Whilst much of Harvey's piece draws upon the experience of the United States, the article by Ursula Huws has an added resonance for British readers, dealing as it does with the privatisation of the state itself, an ongoing process we are presently enduring. If privatisation is allowed to wrap its tentacles further around health provision, care of the disabled and the elderly, combined with the constant political clamour to cut our cloth to match our purse, it is only to be expected that eventually there will be moves towards a fully tiered system of provision with 'top-up payments' and only a basic service free. Both the Conservative and New Labour governments have proved innovators, within the neo-liberal paradigm, starting with direct privatisation of the utilities, moving on to the private finance initiative, compulsory competitive tendering, academies and 'free schools', and now for the finale – the privatisation of state institutions and, in particular, the NHS, itself a living example of a highly effective un-marketised non-capitalist enterprise. As the author puts it, within this shrinking state its purpose will be no longer to deliver services but merely to procure them, and she quotes the example of Suffolk County Council which is trying to put theory into practice by plans to reduce their present 27,000 staff to 300. There is, of course, the necessary ideological smokescreen, the rhetoric of the 'big society' and the 'empowerment' of local communities through truncated undemocratic membership dispensations; for example, foundation hospitals, and allowing charities to take over previous welfare functions of the state. The author observes that there is disagreement within the élite between those who are happy to have a large state, as long as it is profit-based, and the minimalists. This is an interesting article and the thinking behind it could be compared with Naomi Klein's idea of 'disaster capitalism'. The author concludes with an appeal for 'new forms of organisation' to combat the 'globally-organised employers'. We could, perhaps, add to this the need for the existing organisations, namely the trade unions, to intensify their attempts to think globally and act locally.

An article by Nicole Aschoff on the collapse and resurrection of the United States' motor industry, and its connection with the credit crunch and the continuing debt crisis, exemplifies the aggressive, amoral nature of modern higher management practice with its ideology of 'creative destruction'. The ability of employers and government to seize the crisis as an opportunity to fulfil their ambitions (which in this case was a dramatic diminution of the power of the United Automobile Workers) and make a drastic reduction in wages and conditions is covered chronologically in detail. The management succeeded in virtually all of its aims and the UAW policy of concessions did nothing to halt the mass redundancies, wage reductions and erosion of benefits. Additionally, the fall in trade union membership was not staunched and non-unionised foreign assembly plants and suppliers have, so far, remained immune to the blandishments of the UAW. Besides struggling to increase unionisation, the author recommends that the autoworkers look to placing themselves in the forefront of 'green technology development' to revitalise their struggle and presumably form an alliance with the powerful environmental movement in North America. The car industry in the US, and it may be a valid perspective for the European and Asian industries, is not to be viewed as one in decline but one of constant reorganisation and adjustment to the market, truly a process of 'creative destruction', but why must the autoworkers always be the victims of the necessary changes?

In this *Register* there are many more enlightening articles on aspects of the current crisis including the new American Poor Law, the contradictions of neo-liberal climate policy, China's position in the current mess, why Latin America has weathered the financial storm better, how Ireland and Eastern Europe have been affected and, perhaps oddly, an article on racial disparity in analytical texts which requires 67 footnotes and familiarity with a lot of US publications which, unfortunately, this reviewer does not possess.

There is a fascinating article on finance, oil and the Arab awakening, explaining the centrality of the Gulf States to American military power and wealth. The peculiar make-up of the population within the Gulf States, with its very high input of migrant labour, has not rendered it immune to the uprising in the Arab world. Although the coverage of such turmoil is hardly mentioned in the Western media, with the exception of Bahrain, savage pre-emptive repression of discontent has been the norm, particularly in Saudi Arabia and Oman. The article concentrates on the symbiotic relationship between the ruling élites of the US and the Gulf States, and the importance of the latter in recycling petrol dollars and world liquidity. For example, the increase in oil prices over the period 2002-6 has earned the Gulf States some *extra* £510 billion out of a worldwide total of £1.02 trillion.

The final three articles are taken up with the Eurozone crisis and what might be the alternatives for the Left in this context. Of course, the reader will be aware that the articles were written in 2011 and this is still, at the time of writing, very much an ongoing crisis. The most substantial of the pieces is by Elmar Altavater, author of *The Limits of Globalisation,* who teaches at the Free University, Berlin. He sees the crisis as one of capital accumulation expressed in the huge imbalances in current accounts between 11 nations in deficit and six in surplus. The crisis follows a pattern: having started in the property sector, it moves to the banks, the banks pass it on to the government as sovereign debt and, finally, the working class is expected to pick up the burden. However, as banks protect their reserves and unemployment and inflation increase, the tax revenue falls and welfare payments increase, thus expanding sovereign debt. For the author 'there are only two paths in Europe right now': the collapse of the Eurozone or, alternatively, moves towards 'European statehood', and both present serious difficulties. He notes in this context the 'monsters' of the drama, the rating agencies, more powerful in influencing events than some governments.

The second article, by Costas Lapavista, sees the Eurozone as a weak link in the chains of capitalism, and capable of being broken if the Left adopts 'radical solutions', ditching the 'Europeanism' of more optimistic Left pundits. Out should go any pretence of converting the Euro into a 'good Euro', and the idea of monetary union should be abandoned as it is not possible to reform in the interest of the working class. Lapavista summarily dismisses issuing Eurobonds through the European Central Bank, commenting that the latter institution 'does not possess a magic wand to make debts disappear'. With this rejection he would appear to be in accord with some Eurozone leaders, Angela Merkel in particular. Possibly, he is not aware of comprehensive proposals made by Stuart Holland to revitalise the EU economy by using the European Investment Bank, which already issues bonds in its own right, as the vehicle for issuing Eurobonds (see *Spokesman 113 and 115*).

The final article, by Michel Husson, suggests that socialists cohere around what he calls 'a strategy of extension'. If a radical government of the Left materialises it would institute changes that might bring it into conflict with other EU states. Such a government would not seek to break up the Eurozone but should be prepared to work outside its rules and, if necessary, be prepared to abandon the common currency. Of course, this is all predicated on the basis that austerity measures illicit a response that transforms the present political map, both nationally and internationally.

As usual, the high standard we have grown to expect from the *Socialist Register* is maintained in what promises to be an interesting year in terms of possible changes. There could be radical change, but it is equally possible that we see an intensification of the trends towards barbarism, with war clouds again gathering in the Middle East. The Western power élite may be faced with an economic crisis, but it shows no signs of changing course from the brutal economics of austerity and the hardly suppressed desire to intervene militarily whenever its interests are questioned. This edition of the *Register* helps us to understand events as they unfold and, hopefully, will help to guide our future actions.

John Daniels

Healthy Prognosis

Steve Brouwer, *Revolutionary Doctors – How Venezuela and Cuba are changing the world's conception of health care*, Monthly Review Press, 240 pages, paperback ISBN 9781583672396, £15

Experience has taught me to be wary of well-meaning liberals from Europe and the USA. They are full of good intentions, but tend to see the reality through rose-tinted spectacles. (To give just one example: most of what you read about 'liberation theology' and 'the preferential option for the poor' is total nonsense.) I approached this book with similar misgivings. For a start, I hate the title. We should get away from the idea of doctors and that they know best! They are not that important, only of marginal use.

So, the book gets off to a bad start and the early chapters don't improve things much: lots of statistics, only of some interest to those with a special interest in the subject, but otherwise pretty boring. I actually have a specialist interest myself, and was still pretty bored. Then things started to look up. Once Mr Brouwer stops talking about health he becomes very interesting. His brief survey and analysis of what has been going on over the last few years in Latin America (and still continues with ever-growing momentum) are superb. So while I might advise you to skip some of the earlier chapters, I highly recommend this book to anyone who has the slightest interest in Latin American and North American politics and, in the end, health, too.

Even as the war criminals in the corridors of power in Washington and European capitals run amok in the Middle East, this book offers some hope. There are cracks appearing in the foundations of the empire of the Great Satan in the North. It used to be poor little Cuba and Nicaragua that got beaten up, but they somehow resisted and survived. Now they are not alone. Other, bigger countries are joining in the act. The visions of Francisco Morazan and Simon Bolivar are beginning to have some kind of reality: the United States of Latin America. There is increasing co-operation between Latin American countries, even to throwing off the yoke of the dollar and having their own monetary system, the Sucre. Of course, the conservative forces of rich oligarchies and fascist military are still around, backed by the United States, the authors of unbelievable repression, 'disappearances' and 'dirty wars' in the past. Their recent coups in Venezuela and Ecuador came to nothing, so they seem to be on the run. Only in Honduras did they succeed, in 2009, but immediately ran into deep trouble, ostracised by most of their neighbours, so much so that they had to subject themselves to a kind of truce with the President they had deposed, brokered by the President of Colombia and their arch-enemy, the loathed Hugo Chavez of Venezuela (full title: La Republica Bolivariana De Venezuela, which is why this book refers to the 'Bolivarian Revolution'. It has nothing to do with Bolivia; it's Venezuelan.)

Mr Brouwer concentrates on the regimes of the Castro brothers in Cuba and Hugo Chavez, but Evo Morales of Bolivia, Rafael Corea of Ecuador, and Daniel Ortega of Nicaragua also get honourable mention, as does the ousted President of Honduras, 'Mel' Zelaya, now back in his country after months in exile trying to build a new Party of Resistance – he has a long way to go. The author could also have mentioned Cristina Hernandez of Argentina, the widow of Nestor Kirchner, and just re-elected, Dilma Rousseff of Brazil, who succeeded Lula Silva, Fernando Lugo, the President of Paraguay, and perhaps even 'Pepe' Mujica of Uruguay. I know little of his politics, but I love him because his image is so different from the average politician's: he looks as if he has just crawled out from under a hedge after spending the night in a field.

The new President of Peru, Ollanta Humala, is still an unknown quantity, as is the President of Haiti, Michel Martelly. I like him, too. Whilst on the campaign trail he danced in front of his audiences, and wiggled his bum to their great delight. (Can you imagine Barak Obama or David Cameron doing that?) Juan Manuel Santos of Colombia is interesting, too. Is he slowly throwing off the Gringo yoke? He maintains close contact with his more radical neighbours. The only lost causes seem to be Mexico, although Andrés Obrador, who was probably defrauded of the Presidency in 2006, is making a come-back, and Chile. Both countries have seen huge, mostly peaceful, demonstrations going on for months on end. They don't seem, so far, to have made much difference.

But back to health, which this book is supposed to be about, for all its superb survey of local, that is to say, Latin American politics. What relevance does it have for UK readers? Quite a lot, I should say. I have no personal knowledge or experience of the Venezuelan health services, though I do of the Cuban, Nicaraguan, Honduran and British ones. The Cuban and Nicaraguan health services provide useful models.

The truth is, sophisticated medicine does not make much difference to mortality or life expectancy. We can only hope in the case of Hugo Chavez, confronting cancer, that it does. He faces his illness with extraordinary courage. He talks about it openly, makes no attempt to hide the ravages of post-operative therapies that have left him looking like Humpty Dumpty, bald as an egg. He remains his old defiant, challenging, articulate self, and may he long continue to be so. But such medicine, admirable as it may be (and very expensive) makes little difference to national health. What makes the difference is hygiene, nutrition and basic back-up services. Both Cuba and Nicaragua are big on general health advice, for example, keep those with diarrhoea well hydrated with drinks you can make up in the house, and with alternative medicines.

Nicaragua is very involved with herbal medicine, as is Cuba, which also pushes homeopathy and floral essences, financing research into both. Mr Brouwer mentions medicinal plants. He could have said more. Having no knowledge of health practices in Venezuela, I don't know. Perhaps there was not much more to say. Yet, if the links between Venezuela and Cuba are as close as he claims, there must be a huge input about alternative medicines. They are cheap, reasonably safe and effective. You don't have to be a rocket scientist or brain surgeon to put them into practice. These, along with proper food, clean water, hygiene and sanitation, plus a little happiness (difficult to measure, but undoubtedly it plays its part) are the ingredients for a longer and healthier life.

Read the book. Skip a few chapters as you will, but it's worth reading. Interested in Latin America? In health? There is something for all of us.

Nigel Potter, Honduras

Activist

Mark Seddon, *Standing for Something: Life in the Awkward Squad*, Biteback Publishing, 258 pages, hardback ISBN 9781849541237, £16.99

Mark Seddon has produced a highly entertaining and instructive account of his many years of life as a political activist, campaigner and journalist. It makes a much more stimulating read than the memoirs of many a New Labour insider. He is proud to declare himself an 'outsider', but did get close enough to provide valuable testimony on how the whole operation worked. In fact, he was once – but only once – invited to join Tony Blair for a chat on his notorious sofa where all key government policies are alleged to have been formed!

Mark became interested in politics as a schoolboy and, to the dismay of his family, joined the Labour Party at the tender age of 15. He soon became an active member of the local party in Devizes, which was close to the minor public school he attended. When he went up to the University of East Anglia he became heavily involved in both student politics and campaigning with the Norwich Labour Party, which was then one of the strongest and most active in the country. He mobilised students to help in local election campaigns and became the Labour Club's candidate for President of the Students' Union at around the time of the great miners' strike of 1984. Seddon led the students in active support of the Durham miners who came to picket East Anglian ports, and visited the Durham and Notts coalfields in solidarity.

In 1993, Seddon's political campaigning and successful journalism won him the editor's job at *Tribune*, the labour leftwing weekly. Nobody knew then that this was on the eve of events that would radically transform the Labour Party and the political process in Britain. John Smith, who had become the popular and consensual leader of the Party, died suddenly and tragically the following spring. He was succeeded by Tony Blair through a deal with Gordon Brown with which we are now all too familiar. Blair quickly set out on the path of 'New Labour' by demolishing Clause 4 and, as only later became fully apparent, carrying forward the Thatcher neo-liberal project for the economy and society at the expense of labour's traditional social democratic aspirations.

Seddon and his Tribune colleagues* were right to be uneasy about what was to come when, on the day after the 1997 Election, they huddled together in their favourite haunt, the Gay Hussar in Soho, while organised flag-waving triumphalism reigned in Downing Street. Pushing through the New Labour project required an ever-tightening stranglehold on the party's policies and institutions by Blair, Brown and – Seddon's principal *bête noire* – Peter Mandelson ('self-serving, egotistical and narcissistic'). But this process all took some time and, while there was still life and spirit in the Party, Seddon managed to get himself elected to the new National Executive Committee on the slate of the Grassroots Alliance with the highest vote.

However, he and his grassroots colleagues were but a small minority on the Executive, and were unable to prevent the purge of the 'awkward squad' members of the European Parliamentary Labour Party like Ken Coates. This was achieved through the introduction of a new closed list system for the 1999 Euro elections in large regional constituencies where only those near the top of the party list had any chance of success. This control by the centre was subsequently extended to national elections by other means. Seddon himself became a victim of this process and, despite local support in winnable constituencies, was only ever permitted to stand in the hopeless Tory seat of Buckingham.

Although Seddon had supported the action against Saddam's invasion of Kuwait, and NATO's later intervention in Kosovo, he was sceptical about further intervention in Iraq and, early on, publicly expressed his doubts about Blair's claims of its possession of weapons of mass destruction. He visited Iraq himself on two occasions and, with the help of George Galloway, managed to secure an exclusive interview with Iraq's veteran foreign minister, Tariq Aziz. Aziz gave assurances about the weapons and asked Seddon to deliver an invitation to the prime minister to come and see for himself. But Blair, along with Alastair Campbell, simply treated Seddon's initiative with derision. Neither was Gordon Brown any more receptive, being preoccupied with Seddon's strong objections to his pet private finance initiative project.

Seddon opposed military action against Iraq without specific United Nations sanction at the Labour Party conference and, subsequently, on the National Executive. But with the whole weight of the government machine, reinforced by 'dodgy dossiers', he and a handful of colleagues (Ann Black, Christine Shawcroft, Dennis Skinner) were unable to prevail. On the eve of the invasion their resolution was ruled out on procedural grounds and Seddon walked out of the meeting.

Soon after, tens of thousands walked out of the Labour Party. The trauma and the tragedy of the war finally knocked the heart out of the Labour Party. Mark Seddon did not quit but I suspect that it was a similar disenchantment that impelled him to seek new pastures. In 2005, he left the National Executive to pioneer a new role for Al Jazeera, the Arabic television station, as their United Nations correspondent in New York. His adventures and encounters in that role provide many fascinating stories and pen pictures of people he encountered in the course of his work, both great and small. His assessments of some of the statesmen and celebrities he met up with or managed to interview are sometimes surprising but always interesting, just as they are when he discusses his experience of some of the heavyweights and not-such-heavyweights of the British Labour movement.

Where does the 16-year rule of Blair and Brown leave the Labour Party? Mark Seddon says that Labour 'gives every impression of not knowing what on earth it stands for' and that it is now extremely difficult for Labour to reconnect with its natural supporters. And yet his 'hunch' is that 'Labour will eventually be radicalised' in opposition. The signs are not too hopeful just now with Ed Miliband surrounded by unreconstructed Blairites and seemingly too timid to develop an independent base. But for the sake of the political health of the nation, to say nothing of social justice, equality and wellbeing, we must hope that Mark's natural optimism will prevail.

Ken Fleet

*One of the *Tribune* diners that day was Martin Rowson who has contributed a foreword and cartoons to this book.

The Commissioner's View

Thomas Hammarberg, *Human Rights in Europe: No grounds for complacency*, Council of Europe Publishing 2011, 370 pages, paperback ISBN 9789287169167, 19 euros

As the Council of Europe Commissioner for Human Rights, Thomas Hammarberg offers an insider's view of what he has witnessed after visiting almost all of the 47 member states of the Council of Europe. After meeting with various politicians, judges, prosecutors and victims of human rights violations, Hammarberg expresses impatience for the lack of passion and resolve to turn human rights principles into reality.

It is only fairly recently that human rights have been formally recognised as fundamental to securing freedom, justice and peace in the world, and it has taken around 70 years to get where we are today. International treaties have been drafted, ratified and implemented, and have sought to protect civil and political rights; economic, social and cultural rights; and the rights of individuals during time of armed conflict. One of the most important international treaties of the previous century, concerning the protection of human rights and fundamental freedoms for individuals in Europe, came into force on 3 September 1953. The European Convention on Human Rights (ECHR) drew inspiration from its predecessor, the Universal Declaration of Human Rights, and sought to attain effective political democracy through the incorporation of what became a traditional civil liberties approach. The additional protocols to the ECHR have also had the effect of expanding the rights that can be protected; but as the closest thing Europe has to a 'Bill of Rights', the ECHR is vitally important to every individual within the jurisdiction of the High Contracting Parties, and must be adhered to. With every member state of the Council of Europe having ratified the ECHR, there is no room, and certainly no grounds, for complacency. Thomas Hammarberg provides an account of the shortcomings that exist in European human rights implementation today, offering recommendations and concrete remedies to tackle this fundamental issue.

Over the years, the ECHR has proven that individuals can indeed challenge High Contracting Parties who are in breach of any of the rights and freedoms afforded under the Convention, with access to effective remedies. This has included breaches of habeas corpus rights, the right to a fair trial and the prohibition of torture (of particular relevance in recent years, where signatories have taken measures derogating from obligations in times of emergency). Even with agreed standards of human rights at European and international level, there is an implementation gap and standards are not consistently enforced.

Of all the circumstances that could delay necessary reforms or even hinder a culture of respect for human rights or the rule of law, the 'war on terror' is at the top of the list. Hammarberg names and shames the European governments that did not defend their citizens from grave human rights violations, allowed unlawful indefinite detention in Guantanamo bay, and were compliant with the CIA's secret abduction tactics – all in the name of national security and counter terrorism. It is rightly argued that terrorism should not be fought with methods that violate human rights, and that this lesson has already been learned through the experiences of Northern Ireland (directing the reader to further useful documentation that highlights the work of cross-community human rights groups).

Hammarberg attributes this hypocrisy and lack of adherence to agreed international human rights standards to a lack of political will – hijacking, distorting and demeaning the importance of these rights in order to use them as propaganda tools against other states for the preservation of national pride. This is particularly relevant to counter-terrorism measures, as well as the existence of xenophobia and lack of identity rights. Even with Europe's multicultural, inherently plural nature, discrimination on the grounds of sexuality, ethnicity, faith, nationality, social class, age, political viewpoint, and many others still exists. Hammarberg argues that states should actively promote fundamental principles of pluralism, tolerance and broad-mindedness on which democracy itself is based, and promotes a platform for representatives of non-dominant groups to create continuous dialogue between groups in order to avoid a widening of the gaps for growing inequalities and injustice. A sound recommendation, followed by more practical measures needed to address discrimination; further issues, such as the European Court of Human Rights' Margin of Appreciation (*marge d'appreciation*), which takes into account cultural, historic and philosophical differences between states in question, could be more fully addressed in order to assess the potential for this concept to be added to the list of excuses for delaying necessary reforms.

Of more recent issues, Hammarberg also discusses human rights in relation to the global economic crisis; socio-economic rights have traditionally not been fully recognised as justiciable in some areas of Europe, and were not incorporated into the ECHR, only later codified in the separate European Social Charter. Again, this is another area of human rights law that has been politicised, with some regarding socio-economic rights as political aspirations to be addressed at the discretion of the individual governments (for example, rights to adequate standards of living, food, education and rights to housing, health and work). The monitoring body of the Social Charter (the European Committee of Social Rights) provides an effective procedure and useful mechanism to support member states in efforts to achieve their duties under the Social Charter. However, as Hammarberg highlights, not even a third of the Council of Europe states have decided to become party to it – furthermore undermining the great advances that have been made.

This book offers a concise overview of the current position of human rights law in Europe today and looks into further issues, such as immigration and asylum policies; the rights of people with disabilities; gender rights; rights of the child, and freedom of expression – each is considered in light of examples with recommendations of further reading for more in-depth understanding. Ultimately, Hammarberg calls for stricter implementation, including systematic measures, rights-oriented budget analysis, more education on human rights, and more stringent measures to ensure that governments and international actors are held accountable for violations of human rights. Any prospect of international peace and security is inextricably linked with a respect for the human rights of others; even with the extensive human rights legislation in existence, state parties can – and certainly do – hold reservations to exclude or modify certain provisions, and it is largely due to arguments surrounding cultural relativism (see, for example, the list of reservations for the Convention on the Elimination of all forms of Discrimination Against Women). As this book highlights, by challenging the current culture of hypocrisy and selective criticism on behalf of governments, human rights can gradually become distinct from politicised rhetoric that can distort and manipulate the meanings behind them. Only then might we be afforded any grounds for complacency.

Stephanie Sampson

A full pdf of this title is available from:
http/www.coe.int/t/commissioner/Viewpoints/ISBN2011 en.pdf

BEN BELLA

*As we go to press, the death of Ahmed Ben Bella, founding President of Algeria, has been announced. We shall publish a full appreciation later. Meanwhile, we reprint the conclusion to **Stuart Holland's** account of his and Ken Coates' role in helping to secure the President's release from house arrest in Algeria in 1980. The full story appears in Spokesman 110 under the title 'Act and Survive'.*

'... Ben Bella made plain that, without Ken's initiative he still could have been at M'Sila, or elsewhere, under house arrest, indefinitely. He paid tribute to Amnesty International, who had published multiple protests against his imprisonment and also then his house arrest, but added: "They did well. They protested. But you acted."

There then followed an event which was Ben Bella's first public appearance in the UK since his release, at the next Labour Party Conference. Understandably, it was packed, not least by many of the Members of Parliament who had signed the early day motion [inviting Ben Bella to London]. Ben Bella spoke in French and I translated. But what he said was prescient rather than only retrospective. Especially when a question was posed: "In prison you learned Arabic and read the Qur'an. Are you now an Islamist?" To which he responded, "I am a Muslim first, an Arab second, and then an Algerian. I am also proud to be an African." There then was a follow-up question from the floor: "And what of the Qur'an?" To which he responded: "My friend, the Qur'an is the inspiration of our faith. It is not a Michelin Guide to the 20th Century." From which now, in a new millennium, many might learn.'

We are all Greeks

The apathy of the rulers of the civilized world to the astonishing circumstance of the descendants of that nation to which they owe their civilization rising as it were from the ashes of their ruin, is something perfectly inexplicable to a mere spectator of the shews of this mortal scene. We are all Greeks. Our laws, our literature, our religion, our arts, have their root in Greece. But for Greece Rome, the instructor, the conqueror, or the metropolis of our ancestors, would have spread no illumination with her arms, and we might still have been savages and idolaters … The human form and the human mind attained to a perfection in Greece which has impressed its image on those faultless productions, whose very fragments are the despair of modern art, and has propagated impulses which cannot cease, through a thousand channels of manifest or imperceptible operation, to ennoble and delight mankind until the extinction of the race.

Percy Bysshe Shelley
Preface to Hellas
composed 1821